LAW FOR PHYSICAL EDUCATORS AND COACHES

GARY NYGAARD, Ed. D.
Professor of Health and Physical Education
The University of Montana

THOMAS H. BOONE, J.D.
Practicing Attorney, Boone, Karlberg and Haddon
Missoula, Montana

BRIGHTON PUBLISHING COMPANY
P.O. Box 6235, Salt Lake City, Utah 84105

Library of Congress Cataloging in Publication Data

Nygaard, Gary , 1941-
    Law for physical educators and coaches.

    Bibliograph: p.
    Includes index.
I. Boone, Thomas H. II. Title.
KF4166.N93   344.73'099   81-38537
ISBN 0-89832-013-5   347.30499   AACR2

ISBN 0-89832-018-6

CONTENTS

PREFACE

In 1972, one of our newspapers reported three sport-related lawsuits on the same day, two of them close to us. This began to revive some heretofore dormant concern because our state had not seen prior active sport litigation. Since then, our concerns have grown along with the increase in these lawsuits and widespread publicity they have received from the media.

For the past five years, the Department of Health and Physical Education at the University of Montana has offered a course on legal issues in physical education and sport. The popularity of this course and the comments of students in it have convinced us that our concerns are shared by many coaches, athletic trainers, and physical educators. These individuals want to know about sport-related lawsuits and they want to know about guidelines the law suggests to reduce the likelihood of their own involvement in a lawsuit.

In this book we provide an overview of important sport injury litigation. We also suggest a number of operational guidelines for those who teach participants in physical activity. We do so in the hope that our comments will help one become that mythical creature, a "reasonable and prudent professional."

1

LEGAL CONCEPTS IN SPORT AND PHYSICAL EDUCATION

1.1 INTRODUCTION

A college student files a lawsuit for $853,000 in damages, in part for the mental anguish of receiving a "D" in a course rather than the expected "A." A Colorado man charges his parents with providing him inhumane and inadequate care as a child and asks for $350,000. A California man sues a would-be companion for standing him up on a date. To avoid a dirty toilet seat, an Arkansas woman attempts to stand on the seat, which then slips, causing her to fall and injure herself. She brings suit. Similarly, a man sues the New York Giants and the New Jersey Sports and Exposition Authority for injuries suffered when spectators push over the portable toilet the man was using in the parking lot at Giant Stadium. Two Washington Redskins fans attempt to use the courts to overturn their team's loss at St. Louis, contending a crucial call in the game violated the rules and robbed the fans of the right to see a victory. A similar charge is filed by Houston Oiler fans after a questionable call in the playoffs following the 1979 season.

People are becoming more lawsuit conscious, filing for greater damages than ever before, even though the allegations made may seem trivial or frivolous. As the last three instances illustrate, lawsuits in sport and physical education are not exempt from this trend.

Since the mid-sixties, sports injury litigation has been increasing. Both criminal and civil litigation occur in sport: the former more notorious, the latter more frequent. In recent years, professional hockey, football, baseball, and basketball players have all been charged with assault. In one of these cases, the injured player asked for $2.65 million and was awarded more than $3.3 million. In a football case, an appeals court held that the intentional infliction of an injury by one player upon another could give rise to tort liability.[1] Noted sports attorney and agent Bob Woolf states:

The Hackbart and Tomjanovich cases carry a very sobering messsage to professional athletes and team front offices. That is, any intentional conduct by a player against another which is outside the rules of play may be answerable in damages against both the player and the team. The cases indicate a more reasonable trend of thinking toward malicious actions which increase only the danger, and not the interest level, in sports. The strong positions taken by the two different courts should, hopefully, serve as an effective deterrent of intentional violence in sports.[2]

Most sport litigation involves a teacher or coach, because most of the responsibility for youth sport programs has been delegated to the public schools. In an article in *Trial* magazine, a practical suggestion made is that attorneys concentrate on the coach's behavior:

The degree of training of the coach or teacher varies from the volunteer Pop Warner coach to the gymnastics instructor with a B.A. in physical education. Whatever the context, however, the coach's experience and maturity exceeds that of his charges. Moreover, in assuming his position, he has assumed responsibility for their safety and well-being. The duty of foreseeing problems, or recognizing situations which may give rise to injury, is inherent in his role and basic to the willingness of parents to entrust their children to his care and to the program which he manages.[3]

Trial listed the following specific duties as common focal points of sports injury litigation:

1. To employ competent coaches, teachers, or referees;
2. To provide safe facilities and properly maintained equipment;
3. To establish procedures and enforce rules concerning proper fitting of uniforms and protective gear, and safe use of equipment.
4. To structure progress with adequate review procedures to assure that participants will not move too rapidly into areas beyond their skills;
5. To select opponents with care to avoid potentially dangerous mismatching;
6. To educate concerning risks in performing a sport when ill or injured and to establish and scrupulously enforce rules regarding reporting of illness or injury;
7. To establish check-up procedures for those who have been ill or injured to assure that illness or injury is no longer an impairing factor.[4]

To illustrate the use of the last two points:

Assume that a high school trampolinist reports to workout with a cold and a stuffy nose. Though the coach had earlier warned his students to always tell him if they were ill or injured, the student does not think his relatively minor illness worth mentioning. While executing a body twist in mid-air, he loses his equilibrium and falls, receiving a serious cervical injury.

Has the coach complied with duty No. 6 in giving the warning which he did? We think not. Thomas Lambert's excellent analysis in 36 ALTA L.J. 1 (1976) of the law concerning the duty to warn in the products liability field sets forth basic principles equally applicable in the sports area. A warning, to be effective practically and legally, must be so disseminated, explained, and enforced as to provide a realistic basis for the expectation that it will prevent the conduct against which it is directed.

The warning in our hypothetical example was insufficient. The coach should have foreseen that such a warning, to be heeded, had to be repeated frequently, with clear explanation of the harm which might result from failure to comply. He should have taken elaborate care to assure that his athletes understood the effect that a modest cold or stuffy nose could have on the intricate balance one needs when he hurls his body twisting through the air.[5]

In addition to the areas listed in *Trial,* sports litigation can cover such broader fields as civil rights, freedom of expression, and due process. Because of the way in which education, and therefore sport, has evolved in our country, the rights of students and teachers are frequently involved in lawsuits in physical education and sport. Let us examine briefly the development of American education and its emphasis on physical activity.

1.2 SPORT AND PHYSICAL EDUCATION
IN AMERICAN EDUCATION

American education derives its basic structure from law, and its basic character from its history. Education is a governmental function delegated to the individual states, who, in turn, establish by statute minimum educational requirements. These requirements are fulfilled under the auspices of local boards of education. Under this system most states require their students to complete a number of credits or clock hours in physical education. The activities included in this required program are quite varied, and it is possible for two neighboring cities each to have a required physical education program but with completely different activities and games. The local control of education permits this diversity. Further, since many states regard intramural and interscholastic athletics as extensions of the physical education program, these activities are also considered to be part of the governmental function of education. To a degree, then, these programs exist because of state law.

The religious origin of American education, along with the development of various gymnastic systems, sports and games, pragmatic and experimental educational philosophies, physical fitness and the search for the active lifestyle, and the entertainment value of interscholastic sports have given an active character to our educational system. We expect students to be active and we hope they will retain or rediscover the joy of play they possessed as children. One of the unique features of American education is the strong emphasis on physical activities, games, and sports. In light of the puritanical origin of public education in the American colonies, such emphasis on "frivolous" activities seems ironic.

Religious Roots of American Education

The impetus for establishing a program of education in the colonies was religious. Most teachers were clergymen, lay readers, or candidates for the ministry. The church played a leading role in the founding of schools and academies, which usually confined their teaching to the four Rs: reading, 'riting, 'rithmetic, and religion. Any mention of play or sport was made in frequent restrictions against such activities, especially in the infamous "blue laws," which still exert an influence over the games we play. The following mid-eighteenth century statute is an example of a blue law (so called because of the color of the paper on which they were printed and not because of the mood they created): "for the better observation and keeping of the Lord's Day, commonly called Sunday," all persons were required to "carefully apply themselves to the duties of religion and piety"; consequently, "no tradesman, artificer, planter, or labourer" could engage "in hunting, fishing, or fowling" or "use any game, sport, or play," on pain of being fined ten shillings.[6] In fact, the laws that established educational systems, particularly in the New England Colonies, are sometimes referred to as "ould deluder" laws, because the purpose of these laws was to prevent the "ould deluder Satan" from keeping people from the knowledge of the Scriptures.

While these early schools regarded sport and play as anathema, it was not long before sporting activities became a vital part of the curricula of these same schools. Indeed, in the 1890s two of the popular indoor games of today, basketball and volleyball, were devised at a school and in a program controlled by the Young Men's Christian Association (YMCA).

The twentieth century has seen a consistent increase in the popularity of sport and physical education programs. Participation in physical activities, both active and vicarious, now involves more people in more sports than ever before. With rare exception, these activities are no longer condemned by religious organizations. Some writers even refer to sport as a religion and as the new opiate of the masses. Even so, some traces of the religious roots of American education remain; particularly in the social expectation of teachers and coaches.

1.3 SOCIAL ROLES OF TEACHERS AND COACHES

There persist today remnants of the religious origins of American education that created, among other things, higher moral expectations of those who teach and coach than of those who engage in other labors. Teachers have traditionally been held to a higher standard of conduct than have other public empoyees and professionals. In one teacher's contract signed in 1915, the teacher promised a number of things, including:

> not to keep company with men; to be home between the hours of 8:00 p.m. and 6:00 a.m. unless in attendance at a school function; not to loiter downtown in ice cream stores; not to leave town at any time without permission of the chairman of the board; and not to get in a carriage or automobile with any man except her father or brother.[7]

Another contract required a teacher to promise:

> not to go out with any young men except insofar as it may be necessary to stimulate Sunday School work; not fall in love; to remain in the dormitory or on the school grounds when not actively engaged in school or church work elsewhere; to sleep at least eight hours each night[8]

While these examples seem extreme and anachronistic, more recent examples are available. These include a female teacher who in 1971 was directed by the superintendent and the high school principal to refrain from wearing a two-piece bathing suit while giving swimming instruction to junior high school boys. In a 1972 case, a coach in a Texas town was dismissed for "failure to meet accepted moral standards of conduct for the teaching profession" because of his association with a waitress in town following a basketball game.[9] While these are exceptional instances, it is folly to disregard the religious roots of American education. They persist, and they influence the job teachers and coaches do, the way they do it, and the standards by which they are judged. When this traditional and conservative element in the educational system is combined with local control of education, the result is inconsistent expectations of the profession. This is frequently illustrated by the example of two similar lawsuits with opposite results. It is also illustrated by the differing expectations communities have for their teachers, doctors, lawyers, businessmen, but especially teachers. Since many teachers are new to a community, either in the sense of being from somewhere else or returning after years of professional training, it is beneficial to them to try to assess their community's expectations, to try to determine what one may and may not do as a professional educator in that locale. It is, for example, quite possible for one community to condemn public drinking of alcohol by teachers, while the very next town expects teachers, particularly those who coach, to visit the tavern and "have one with the boys." The line between condonation and condemnation may indeed by thin.

1.4 THE LEGAL STRUCTURE OF EDUCATION

Education is not expressly mentioned in the Constitution of the United States. The Tenth Amendment does state that "the powers not delegated to the United States by the Constitution, nor prohibited by it to the States, are reserved to the States respectively, or to the people." The legal responsibility for public education lies with state government, and the states have almost complete responsibility for and control of their public school systems.

Under most state constitutions, the state legislature is authorized to provide public education for its citizens. The state legislature must respect the rights and protections granted to citizens under the federal Constitution when providing public education. Each state may, therefore, choose the kind, form, and scope of its public school system, but whatever education is offered must be consistent with the constitutionally protected rights of any citizen.[10]

State law determines the certification of teachers for public schools, and while the parties in the schooling process are citizens, legal and educational institutions have over the years blurred the citizenship rights of juveniles and teachers. It has taken recent United States Supreme Court decisions to clarify that students and teachers do not shed their constitutional rights at the schoolhouse door and that teachers, in addition to being school employees, are also citizens with the right to exercise the privileges of citizenship.

State governments can organize public education in a variety of ways, but they usually do so by the creation of several school districts. These school districts are managed by elected or appointed school boards with broad management powers and duties. The local school board generally decides what kind of education is offered in the district and typically has powers that include teacher employment, supervision, and dismissal; curriculum design that is consistent with any state-mandated subjects or specific courses; pupil management policies; and determining the school calendar, the scope and nature of the extra-curricular program, the social activities, and so forth.[11] For most practical purposes, the local school board is the functional level of American education. Schools operate at the pleasure of the state legislatures, under sanction of state laws, and within the purview of federal laws; but the organization, management, and operational decisions are left to local school districts under the legal control of the local school board or other governing body.

1.5 SPORT IN THE CURRICULUM

It is within this legal structure, with its conservative and fundamentalist background, that the states prescribe the subjects to be studied — the essence of their educational system. States provide the broad framework of curricular inclusions, and local school districts make more specific determinations as to the disciplines within their educational programs. Nearly all states have a minimum requirement for instruction in health and physical education, usually expressed in a certain number of clock hours per week, semester, or year. In addition, the intramural and extramural programs of schools are regarded as logical extensions of the physical education program. This, together with the strong tradition of interscholastic athletics that developed in the late nineteenth and early twentieth centuries in the United States, places a large segment of the youth sports program within the structure of American public education. This arrangement is somewhat unique and not universally accepted, as Thorstein Veblen's comment on interscholastic sport (albeit large-scale interscholastic sport) illustrates. He said "the relationship of college football to physical culture is much the same as that of bullfighting to agriculture."[12] Nevertheless, the presence of sport in American educational institutions is common enough to be a characteristic of our educational system as illustrated by the federal district court opinion in Moran v. *School District No. 7, Yellowstone County:*

> the present Montana Supreme Court has recognized the importance of extracurricular activities as an integral part of the total education process. Courts have begun to recognize that extracurricular activities such as football are "generally recognized as a fundamental ingredient of the educational process." . . . Thus it is apparent that the right to attend school includes the right to participate in extracurricular activities.[13]

The opinion rendered in *Moran* is the rule, not the exception, that most athletic programs in our schools are justified, at least on the superficial level, as extensions of the physical education program. They are also justified philosophically. At some time during their professional course-work, physical education students are exposed to the pyramid illustrated in Figure 1.1.

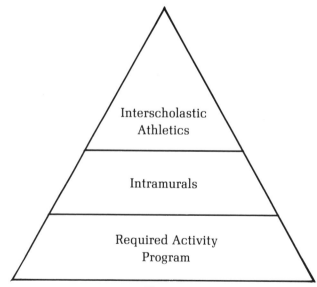

Fig. 1-1.

The theory is that a strong (usually required) activity program involving all of the students will encourage a large portion of the students to enter the intramural program and those with outstanding skills to enter the interscholastic athletic program. While the practical application of this pyramid is and has been in question (and may be inverse), the concept of it is still tendered to students.

In summary, sport in American education is regarded as a legitimate extension of physical education programs. Most states have required minimums for instruction in physical education, to which may be added any extra instruction in the discipline that a local school board may feel is desirable. The control of these physical education, intramural, and sport programs is on a local and state level, so long as no federally guaranteed constitutional rights are violated. Within this legal environment, there exists for those who teach and coach in a community a myriad of local social expectations, which are a remainder and a reminder of the religious origins of American education. To one who chooses to teach and coach, all of this means that one may be expected to exhibit a high moral character, perhaps higher than could be legally enforced in a given community. It is within this environment that sport instruction occurs; and an understanding of this environment can aid one in understanding the legal duties of those who teach and coach.

1.6 THE NATURE OF LEGAL CONCERN IN SPORT AND PHYSICAL EDUCATION

Sport and law have been intertwined for at least hundreds of years. It is not the newness of the relationship that concerns those who teach and coach but its changing nature. In the past, it was not uncommon to hear of a particular sport being banned outright. One can find frequent references to the banning of the game of golf in England in time of military emergency, because the game took time away from practice with the longbow. Many other sports, especially those with an early professional aura (and hence those sports upon which others gambled) were frequently banned. Mention has been made of the blue laws, which banned sports and diversions on the Sabbath. By threat of outlawing the sport, President Roosevelt was instrumental in changing the nature of college football so that the sport was not so brutal. Mention has also been made of the state and locally mandated curriculum, usually including required instruction in physical education and sport activities. The list of general legal involvement in sport is extensive, but it is no longer general involvement that concerns teachers and coaches.

Physical educators and coaches have become more aware of and concerned about the specific legal responsibilities associated with their profession. This concern developed because of the increase in the number of lawsuits in physical education and sport, the size of the monetary settlements in these suits, and the close judicial inspection of professional behavior, frequently by a jury consisting of nonprofessionals. The concern is apparent and understandable. According to data collected by the American Mutual Insurance Association, 43 percent of all judgments in 1965 went to the plaintiff, with an average award of $11,644. By 1973, the percentage of judgments in favor of the plaintiff came to 54 percent with the average award at $79,940.[14] At this writing, the manufacturers of football helmets are involved in product liability lawsuits totalling more than $100 million in claims. People are more likely to sue today, and the amounts requested are frightening. The high percentage of student injuries which occur in physical education and sport programs (67 percent boys, 59 percent girls) makes these programs attractive targets for lawsuits. Most of these lawsuits are based on negligence, in which there are claimed to be breaches of legal duties. Most lawsuits, therefore, involve an examination of the manner in which a physical education teacher or coach did or did not carry out a legal duty.

Judges and juries are examining the methods by which specific techniques in play, games, and sports are taught in schools. Attention is now focused more on the manner in which a sport is conducted than on the appropriateness of the sport (unless a school happens to include such a sport as cockfighting in its curriculum). Judges and juries are now focusing on such factors as the appropriateness of an outdoor shuttlecock being used indoors; the state of mind of a student at the time of injury; the validity of syllabi used for lesson plans, as in teaching line soccer to girls when it is listed in the curriculum guide as an activity for boys; the method of teaching tackling; the absence of face masks in softball; the absence of a knob on the end of a softball bat; and even the scheduling of a varsity football team against an obviously superior team. Three-wheeled golf carts may be hazardous, and it may be necessary to specify that the numbers indicating depth in a swimming pool be in feet, not meters. Unfortunately, this legal scrutiny of method and manner has not been consistent. An action or decision held to be reasonable and prudent in one case has not been held to be so in another. As a result, physical educators and coaches must try to balance fun with safety and learn to teach skills to students safely, while keeping the activities enjoyable.

Most educators are impressed and undoubtedly concerned about the size of awards in sport litigation. Several cases illustrate the severity of this problem. They are presented chronologically and, admittedly, are used herein for their shock value. In 1958 a football player was injured during a scrimmage. There was some confusion over the means of transportation and consequent movement, and the player became paralyzed. He was awarded $207,000, a very large award for its time, especially in a school sport lawsuit.[15] In 1964 a student in a high school gymnastics class was injured when he attempted a stunt while the teacher was attending to another student. As a result of the injury, the student was paralyzed. He was awarded $1,216,000 which was later reduced to $335,140.[16] In 1975 a sixteen-year-old football player broke his neck and became a permanent quadriplegic when he attempted to tackle an opponent. The injury returned an award of $5.3 million, plus an additional amount for medical expenses.[17] At the 1979 American Alliance for Health, Physical Education and Recreation Convention, one paper presented was entitled "Could You Pay a $147,000,000 Settlement?[18] This was the possible sum of damages in a case involving an injury in a swimming pool accident. These numbers, while exceptional, are publicized and increase the concerns of the physical education teachers and coaches about their specific responsibilities, how they carry them out, and how they can protect themselves in the event of a student injury and subsequent lawsuit.

In addition to the social expectations of teachers, the frequency of lawsuits, the size of awards, and the close scrutiny of their professional actions, one other problem has complicated the instruction of athletic and physical education skills. This is the tendency to bring suit against anyone involved with an incident, no matter how remote the involvement. For example, in approximately one-third of the product liability suits involving a manufactured piece of athletic equipment, the coach or physical education teacher is named as codefendant along with the manufacturer and seller.

Many teachers and coaches, when appraised of the increase in sport injury litigation, tend to protect themselves from the problem by avoiding it—the "head in the sand" or "ignorance is bliss" approach. This, of course, could prove to be disastrous, as ignorance is a notoriously poor defense in a lawsuit. It seems imperative that those who teach and coach develop, as a part of their professional training, a basic understanding of legal concepts as they apply to educators, as well as a practical understanding of the extent and limitations of their professional responsibilities. It is the purpose of this text to introduce prospective teachers and coaches to this topic.

1.7 THE LEGAL DUTIES OF PHYSICAL EDUCATION TEACHERS AND COACHES

The legal duties of teachers and coaches are not always consistent. They vary from place to place and from time to time. It would be impossible to present a thorough discussion of this topic with concrete guidelines which would protect everyone from injury and subsequent lawsuit. There are risks inherent in any physical activity, and this has made the gymnasium and the playing field the location of injuries and the source of lawsuits. According to one source, 67 percent of all school jurisdiction accidents involving boys and 59 percent involving girls occur in physical education and recreation programs.[19] Underlying the following discussion is the need for anyone who teaches or coaches movement activities to minimize the probability of injury, particularly injuries due to factors extraneous to the activity.

It must be emphasized that a participant should be exposed only to those risks inherent in a sport. Two skiing cases illustrate this point. In a 1951 case, the plaintiff, an experienced skier, hit a snow-covered stump and fractured her leg while on an intermediate trail.[20] The court ruled that the danger of encountering a snow-covered stump was an inherent risk of skiing. However, a 1978 Vermont case awarded $1,500,000 to a twenty-one-year-old novice skier.[21] The novice's skis became entangled in a clump of brush three to four feet in from the edge of a novice trail. The Vermont Supreme Court emphasized that the risk of encountering brush on the trail was not an inherent danger of the sport. The court rejected the defense of assumption of risk, distinguishing between injuries sustained in the sport rather than the condition of the area provided for the sport. The court concluded that not every fall was inherent in the sport.

The remainder of this text will present general guidelines for safer teaching and coaching of physical education and sport activities. The tone of this discussion will be cautious, on the assumption that it is generally better to err on the conservative side if one is to err at all. This does not imply that teaching or coaching need prohibit risk or prohibit fun. It does imply that the risk allowed should be part of the activity taught, and that fun should not rule the activity but should be contained within the rules of the activity.

There are at least five duties of a physical education teacher or coach. Each of these duties is made up of a number of additional minor duties. *The first of these legal duties is that of providing a safe environment.* This implies prior planning with regular and thorough inspection of all facilities and areas to be used. The standard of care to which one is now held is that of a reasonable and prudent *professional.* A reasonably prudent teacher or coach should possess the skill and take the time to examine the teaching/coaching station and should remove those hazards which create an unreasonable risk not inherent in the activity. It is important to develop a "sport-specific" concept while carrying out these legal duties. Thus, as one inspects the teaching area to be used, the guidelines for examining the area must consider what activity is to be taught, what common risks there are in that activity, where common risks are likely to occur with this activity on this teaching station, and what must be done to reduce the potential severity of these common risks, these sport-specific risks.

A second category of legal duty is in the area of planning. The major emphasis is on the immediate short-term plans teachers and coaches make as they go about their daily duties, those duties that are closest to their supervisory responsibilities.

A third legal duty, and probably the most important one, is the duty to supervise. This duty has two important facets, general and specific supervision, and each sport or movement activity has the potential need for both. It is the responsibility of the teacher or coach to develop sound techniques for general supervision and to develop an awareness of the need for and a means of immediately applying specific supervision for the activity being taught.

A forth category of legal duties pertains to those duties which occur once an injury or accident has taken place. There have been several tragic cases involving improper emergency procedures; it is essential that a teacher or coach understand his or her role and responsibilities in the event of injury. Essential are the abilities to apply first aid, to communicate with other emergency personnel, and to arrange the safe transportation of the injured. All of these should be a part of a school emergency plan in which each teacher and coach is sure of his or her role.

A *final category of legal duty pertains to record keeping.* While this is the least emphasized of the legal duties, it is important to know what records are necessary, how long they must be kept, and what information they should contain.

1.8 NARRATIVE OF LEGAL TERMS

The following contains most of the legal terms used in this text. Other terms will be introduced either in the glossary at the end of this chapter or in appropriate later chapters. In general, it is important to remember that most actions involving physical education teachers and coaches are civil actions and do not involve criminal charges. Most lawsuits in physical education and sport occur in the section of *tort* law called *negligence*. A tort is not easily defined, indeed Prosser's textbook on tort law devotes the better part of the first chapter to defining a tort.[22] A tort is considered to be:

A *wrong* done to another person; a *civil* (as opposed to criminal) wrong that does not involve a *contract*. For an act to be a tort, there must be: a legal duty owed by one person to another, a breach of that duty, and harm done as a direct result of the action.[23]

The last part of the above definition is very similar to the operational definition of negligence, that is, the four factors necessary to prove negligence are listed. *Negligence* is the failure to exercise a reasonable or ordinary amount of care in a situation that causes harm to someone or something. Negligence can:

involve doing something carelessly or failing to do something that should have been done. Negligence can vary in seriousness from gross (recklessness or willfulness) through ordinary (failing to act as a reasonable careful person would) to slight (not much).[24]

In the context of physical education and sport, negligence would be the *failure to perform a legally owed duty* as would a reasonable and prudent professional (teacher, coach), with this failure resulting in *actual damage* that is *causally related* to the *breach of duty* and that should have been foreseen.

Most lawsuits in physical education and sport are negligence suits. There are exceptions which should be mentioned, but because they rarely occur, they need not be emphasized. One of these exceptions is an occasional *criminal* charge brought because of a particularly violent act, usually, thus far, during a hockey game. Hockey players who have attacked opponents with a hockey stick have been charged with criminal assault and battery. The other type of legal action that is becoming more common is a lawsuit for *breach of contract* initiated by coaches, players, and teams with long-term contracts that have not been fulfilled.

Negligence lawsuits are usually brought against the teacher, the coach, and the school district. Until recently, it was difficult to sue a school district successfully because of *sovereign immunity* for the governmental entity, and thus the brunt of the lawsuit was borne by the *agent* of the school district charged with immediate supervision and his superiors. For years, sovereign immunity from lawsuit has been defended because of a variety of reasons, including the judgment that one has no right against the authority that makes the law on which that right depends, the judgment that an agent of the state who commits a tort is engaged in *ultra vires* actions (outside the scope of his authority), the judgment that public funds should not be used to compensate private parties, and the judgment that it is impossible for the government (*all* the people) or an agency thereof to commit a wrong. The umbrella of sovereign immunity has been reduced and in some states eliminated by a variety of means, including constitutional amendment, legislation, or judicial decision.

The doctrine of *respondeat superior,* by which the employer is responsible for the actions of an employee done in the course of employment, was applied to schools in California in 1943 and has led to the passage of so-called *save harmless* legislation. Under this legislation schools can reimburse employees sued for negligence while employed by the school district, and in some states purchase insurance for the compensation of those injured by a school employee's negligent acts. Other considerations that have reduced the shield of governmental immunity include the distinction between governmental and proprietary functions, mandatory and permissive duties, and ministerial and discretionary duties. From all this, governmental immunity has generally been limited or removed, allowing school districts, among others, to be sued.

The duty of *general* and *specific* supervision is present in any of the following relationships; teacher-student, coach-player, and leader-participant. The teacher, coach, or leader must act in relation to the child as the reasonably prudent parent would *(in loco paren-*

tis), protecting the child from dangers and preventing the child from engaging in self-injury and irresponsibilites. This normally involves general supervision. In the conduct of an activity, a more specific duty is owed to the participant to conduct such activity as would a *reasonable* and *prudent* professional or trained person in that field. There are three other categories of individuals to whom supervisory duties, usually general, may be owed. These include invitees, licensees, and trespassers. An *invitee* is one who is on the premises by invitation for his or her own purposes and for purposes for which the facility or area was established. A *licensee* is a person who is privileged to enter upon the property by virtue of the possessor's consent. A *trespasser* has no consent, *actual* or *implied*, to use the property. If a trespasser is discovered but remains on the premises, he or she does so with the implied consent of the owner and therefore becomes a licensee. The owner of a property must exercise reasonable care for the protection of invitees, including warning of the invitees of dangers which are known and also inspecting the premises to discover possible defects and hazards. Less duty is owed a licensee. Reasonable care must be used to discover the licensee and avoid injury to him or her in carrying out activities on the owner's property, and reasonable care must be taken to warn the licensee of any concealed, dangerous conditions or activities known to the owner, or of any changes in the condition of the premises which may be dangerous. No duty is owed a trespasser. In addition, care must be taken with facilities or equipment that may be an *attractive nuisance*, that is, a condition, piece of equipment, or apparatus that is attractive to young children and dangerous to them because of their inexperience and inability to appreciate danger.

If one is sued for negligence, there are four usual defenses. The first of these is to attempt to prove that any one of the four major elements of negligence was not present: that a legal duty was not present, that there was no breach of a legal duty, that there was no actual damage, or that there was no causal connection between the action and the damage. The defendant's action must have been a substantial factor in the injury; it must have been a proximate cause of the injury. Second, there is no liability present when the proximate cause of an injury is an *act of God* (due to the forces of nature). Third, a plaintiff may be guilty of *contributory negligence*, or conduct on his or her part which contributes as a legal cause to the harm suffered. In some states, negligence by both the plaintiff and the defendant must be compared, and any damages awarded to the

plaintiff awarded on a proportionate basis. The fourth common defense is the *assumption of risk.* This defense means that an element
of risk is always inherent in movement activities, such as are found in
physical education, intramurals, and athletics. If a student knows,
understands, and appreciates these risks, and proceeds to engage in
the activity, the student assumes those risks. Two examples illustrate
the successful use of this defense. In the first, a thirty-five-year-old
man was bouncing on a trampoline at a commercial trampoline center
when he fell and was injured.[25] A trial court ruled in favor of the
plaintiff. The ruling was reversed by the Supreme Court, and the
assumption of risk defense was granted insofar as the court found
that the signs posted, a lack of hidden danger, and signs telling
patrons to ask for instructions if desired, were sufficient to warn a
thirty-five-year-old plaintiff.

Other cases have examined the plaintiff's age, education, and
intelligence in holding for assumption of risk. In a 1951 case, a
fourteen-year-old fell and broke his arm while attempting to vault
over a gymnasium horse.[26] Based on the plaintiff's testimony, the
court concluded that he was fully aware of the dangers implicit in
this form of exercise and was sufficiently intelligent to be aware of
the potential harm. This was adequate, according to the court, to
compel a finding of assumption of risk.

Several states have adopted the doctrine of *comparative negligence,* under which the degree of negligence of the parties is
compared. Contributory negligence, if only slight, does not become a
complete bar to recovery but generally will reduce the damages
according to the degree of negligence on the part of the plaintiff in
relation to that of the defendant.

1.9 GLOSSARY OF SELECTED LEGAL TERMS*

Act of God   An event caused entirely by nature alone. An unfor-
seeable or unavoidable accident due to forces of nature. For example,
without warning, lightning strikes a golfer on a golf course.

Actual notice/constructive notice   Notice refers to the knowledge of
certain facts. Actual notice is the knowledge of such facts; constructive

---

* A good source of legal definitions for lay people is available in the *Law
Dictionary for Non-Lawyers* by Daniel Oran (St. Paul: West Publishing Co.,
1975).

notice means that a person *should have known* certain facts and will be treated as if he or she knows them. For example, a physical education teacher's awareness of loose floor plates for the horizontal bar is actual notice; if the teacher is not aware of the loose floor plates, her or she should have been aware of them as a result of a regular and thorough inspection of the horizontal bar apparatus.

Assumption of risk   This is one of the common defenses in a negligence suit. It is the acceptance by participants of the fact that an element of risk is inherent in most physical education activities, and if one knows, understands, and appreciates this element of risk and voluntarily participates in the activity, one's chances of collecting damages in the event of an injury are greatly reduced. It is now necessary to not only create an awareness of the inherent risks, but to do so to the degree that students know, understand, and appreciate these risks.

Attractive nuisance   Under this legal principle, if a person keeps dangerous property that is both attractive and accessible to young children, then that person is responsible even if the children are at fault when they get hurt. For example, an unsupervised trampoline is set up and available in a gymnastics area that is accessible to young children. As such it may be an attractive nuisance.

Breach of contract   The failure to perform any promise or to carry out the terms of a contract, without legal excuse.

Business pursuits clause   A clause that may be appended to one's homeowner's policy providing insurance in the event one is sued while carrying out the duties of one's occupation, profession, or business. This is one of the more inexpensive means of carrying liability protection.

Civil action/criminal action   Civil action is a lawsuit that is brought to enforce a right or to gain payment for a wrong. In general, it is a lawsuit brought by one person against another. Most actions in physical education and sport are civil actions. A criminal action is concerned with violation of a government's penal laws and may result in imprisonment, not just damages. A few well-publicized criminal charges have been made in professional hockey and professional football.

Class action   A lawsuit brought for all the persons involved in the same situation. For example, a lawsuit brought by yourself on behalf of yourself and your neighbors alleging that the presence of a lighted softball field is a nuisance would be a class action lawsuit.

Comparative negligence   The relative negligence on the part of both plaintiff and defendant. Any damages awarded are awarded on a proportionate basis.

Contributory negligence   This is another common defense in a lawsuit. It states that there was negligence on the part of the plaintiff which reduces (see *comparative negligence*) or eliminates the negligence attributed to the defendant. For example, the ignoring of warnings and safety procedures by a student in a swimming pool area may contribute to the injury, and may be judged as contributory negligence.

Corporal punishment   Any kind of physical punishment. A teacher who spanks a student for his misdeeds is using corporal punishment.

Defendant   The person against whom a legal action is brought. This action is started by the plaintiff.

Discretionary duty/ministerial duty   A discretionary duty is one carried out by a public official while setting policy. It involves the judgment or discretion of the official, and in the past these public officials frequently had the protection of governmental immunity. Ministerial duties are those duties which are established for and required of employees. No judgment or discretion on the part of the employee is expected, and no governmental immunity exists. Most teachers and employees of a school district are engaged in ministerial duties.

Due process   The fundamental rights accorded parties under our system of jurisprudence.

Duty   This is a legal obligation to another person. For example, if you see an injured person, you may have a moral but not a legal duty to help that person. If you choose to help that person you then have a legal duty to do so as a reasonable and prudent person would.

Foreseeability   That which a reasonably prudent person would perceive and anticipate as a result under existing circumstances.

Good Samaritan laws   These are laws designed to protect one who assumes a legal duty to help another in distress by reducing the legal obligation of the good Samaritan.

Governmental function/proprietary function   This is a distinction sometimes made when examining the role of a governmental agency such as a public school. This distinction was frequently made in an attempt to reduce governmental immunity. In essence, the governmental function of the public school is to educate the young people of a state. When a school chooses to participate in an activity that may be beyond this basic function and involves a fee or spectators (as with athletics), the school may be charged with carrying out a proprietary function rather than or in addition to the governmental function.

Guest statutes   These are laws in some states that do not permit a person who rides in another person's car as a guest (without payment or other business purpose) to sue that person if there is an accident unless the accident involves more than ordinary negligence. However, many states have abolished the requirement that more than ordinary negligence be shown in a guest situation.

In loco parentis   Acting as a parent with respect to the care and supervision of a child. This is a standard of care that teachers, especially of young children, have as a charge. The effect of *in loco parentis* has diminished in recent years.

Last clear chance doctrine   The person who has the last clear chance to avoid damage or injury is the responsible party. This is better understood, perhaps, by example. The last clear chance doctrine was considered in a 1972 Washington case.[27] The plaintiff argued that his gymnastics instructor had the last clear chance to prevent him from falling off a trampoline because the instructor could have stopped the plaintiff from using the trampoline after class had ended. The court, however, held that the last clear chance doctrine applies where the defendant actually sees the plaintiff's peril and can appreciate the danger but fails to exercise reasonable care to avoid injury. The court found no evidence that the plaintiff was in any danger when the instructor observed him. As to the last clear chance doctrine, the court held that the plaintiff had a better chance to avoid the injury because he could have gotten off the trampoline. In addition, by the time the defendant was in a position to witness the plaintiff's peril, he did not have time to prevent the injury.

Liability   A liability is a broad term for legal responsibility, obligation, or debt.

Malfeasance   This is wrongdoing; committing an illegal act. It is to be distinguished from *misfeasance*, which is the improper doing of an otherwise proper act, and from *nonfeasance*, which is the failure to do an act that should have been done. These are errors of commission and omission and are negligent acts.

Negligence   The failure to exercise a reasonable or ordinary amount of care in a situation resulting in harm to someone or something. Negligence can vary from gross negligence (recklessness or willfulness) to ordinary negligence (failure to act as a reasonably careful person would) to slight negligence (very little failure). There are a number of elements to negligence, including a duty owed to another, a breach of the standard of care owed another, damage, and proximate cause between the breach and the resulting injury or damage. These four elements must be proven for negligence to be found.

Nuisance   This is anything persistent or ongoing that annoys or disturbs unreasonably, hurts a person's use of his or her property, or violates the public health, safety, or decency.

Respondeat superior   A legal rule that the employer is responsible for the legal actions of an employee done in the course of employment. This is one of the actions that reduced the umbrella protection of governmental immunity for school districts.

Safe premises   This is the responsibility of schools, among others, to regularly and thoroughly inspect for hazards, warn of hazards, and repair hazards as soon as possible. This duty is designed to protect:

> *invitees*—those persons, such as students, invited onto the premises for a specific purpose. To these invitees, the highest standard of care is owed.
>
> *licensees*—those on the premises with consent of the owner, for example, concessionaires. Licensees must be warned of any hidden hazardous conditions and of any changed conditions that may be hazardous.
>
> *trespassers*—those on the premises without consent. No duty is owed a trespasser, but if one has been trespassing with the knowledge of the owner of the premises, that person may be regarded as a licensee with the above duty.

Save harmless legislation   Legislation that allows or requires a governmental agency such as a school district to purchase insurance to protect its employees from lawsuit, or to reimburse employees for any losses from lawsuit.

Sovereign immunity   The government's freedom from being sued for damages in all but a few special situations where it consents to suit by passing statutes allowing suit.

Standard of care   This has traditionally been held to be behaving as a reasonable and prudent person would behave in the same situation. In lawsuits involving coaches and teachers, it requires behavior that a reasonable and prudent professional would use under the circumstances.

Substantial factor test   The test of whether the alleged action or inaction of the defendant was a significant element in the injury that occurred. As with the proximate cause test, the purpose is to establish a causal relationship between the action or inaction and the injury.

Supervision   The broad term implies the responsibility for the area and for the activities that take place in that area. Two kinds of supervision may be required. *General supervision* refers to the responsibility for planning and conducting the activities as safely as possible. *Specific supervision* has the same element, but because of the nature of the activity it also requires one to supervise closely the conduct of that activity. For example, it is generally sufficient for a playground to have general supervision, but if one of the pieces of equipment on the playground is a trampoline, that trampoline, because of the increased risk it offers, needs to be closely supervised.

Tinker test   This term sometimes used to refer to *Tinker v. Des Moines Independent School District,* 393 U.S. 503, in which it was determined that a "material and substantial disruption" of the educational function of the school must occur or be likely to occur before some thing or some action can be banned by school authorities.

Tort   A private or civil wrong (noncontractual) against another.

Ultra vires Act   An action that is outside the scope of responsibility and authority of an individual. A coach who attempts to relocate a dislocated thumb may be engaged in an *ultra vires* act.

Waiver   The voluntary giving up of a right, as with waiver forms and waiver slips (which sometimes waive little if any).

NOTES

1. Robert G. Woolf, "Courts Coming Down Hard on Excessively Violent Players," *National Law Journal,* January 7, 1980, p. 20.
2. Ibid.

3. Samuel Langerman and Noel Fidel, "Responsibility Is Also Part of the Game," *Trial* 13, no. 1 (January 1977): 23.

4. Ibid., p. 24.

5. Ibid.

6. Oscar Theodore Barck and Hugh Talmage Lefler, *Colonial America* (New York: Macmillan, 1958), pp. 379-380.

7. David Rubin, *The Rights of Teachers* (New York: Avon Books, 1968), p. 109.

8. Ibid.

9. Ibid.

10. William Hazard, Lawrence D. Freeman, Stephen Eisdorfer, and Paul Tractenbery, *Legal Issues in Teacher Preparation and Certification* (Washington D.C.: ERIC Clearinghouse on Teacher Education, 1977), pp. 3-5.

11. Ibid.

12. Thorstein Veblen, *The Theory of the Leisure Class* (New York: Mentor Books, 1953), pp. 173-174. (Originally printed in 1899).

13. *Moran v. School District #7, Yellowstone County,* 350 F. Supp. 1180 (D. Mont. 1972).

14. "Here Is What Liability Responsibility Means for Athletes," *Athletic Purchasing and Facilities,* August 1977, pp. 13-17.

15. *Welch v. Dunsmuir Joint Union High School District,* 326 P. 2d 633 (Cal. App. 1958).

16. *Miller v. Cloidt and Board of Education of the Borough of Chatham,* No. L 7241-62 (N.J. Super. Ct. 1964.

17. Herb Appenzeller, "Sports in the Courts," United States Sports Academy *Newsletter* 1, no. 2 (1978): 4-5.

18. Betty van der Smissen, "Could You Pay a $147,000,000 Settlement?" (Paper presented at ARAPCS General Session, AAHPER Convention, New Orleans, Louisiana March 16, 1979).

19. Charles A. Bucher, *Administration of Health and Physical Education Programs,* 5th ed. (St. Louis: C.V. Mosby, 1971), p. 513.

20. *Wright v. Mt. Mansfield Lift,* 96 F Supp. 786 (D. Vt. 1951).

21. *Sunday v. Stratton Corp.* 136 Vt. 293, 390 A.2d 398, (1978).

22. William L. Prosser, *Law of Torts,* 4th ed. (St. Paul: West Publishing Co., 1971).

23. Daniel Oran, *Law Dictionary for Non-Lawyers* (St. Paul: West Publishing Co., 1975).

24. Ibid.

25. *Daniel v. S-Co Corp.,* 255 Iowa 869, 124 N.W.2d 522 (1963).

26. *Sayers v. Ranger,* 83 A.2d 775 (N.H. Super. Ct. 1951).

27. *Chatman v. State,* 6 Wash. App. 316, 492 P.2d 607 (Wash. Ct. App. 1972).

2

THE RIGHTS OF STUDENTS AND TEACHERS

In chapter 1 we discussed the religious roots of American education and emphasized that some traces of these religious origins remain. Nowhere is this more evident than in the varying expectations for student and teacher behavior. As a rule, the rights of citizenship extend into the school and apply to teachers and students. These rights are subject to the same limits and restrictions in schools as elsewhere, and the assertion of personal rights by teachers and students must not create a material and substantial disruption of the educational process of the school.

2.1 SOURCES OF STUDENT AND TEACHER RIGHTS

The tradition in the United States of compulsory, universal education through a system of free, public schools implies that education is available to all. Very few societies other than our own attempt to create and implement such a broad educational scheme relevant to all. The public schools have the responsibility for the socialization and the emotional, physical, and intellectual development of all our young people. The schools, the teachers, and the students are among the most visible of community institutions and members. Problems and issues of concern in local schools become the problems and issues of concern in the community. Recently, schools have borne the brunt of social unrest, particularly in the area of civil rights.

The civil rights issues raised in the school come from three primary sources. The First Amendment to the Constitution states that "Congress shall make no law respecting an establishment of religion, or prohibiting the free exercise thereof; or abridging the freedom of speech." The Fifth Amendment to the Constitution states that "No person . . . shall be compelled in any criminal case to be a witness against himself, nor be deprived of life, liberty, or property, without due process of law." The Fourteenth Amendment states that "no state shall make or enforce any law which shall abridge the privileges or immunities of citizens of the United States; nor shall any state deprive any person of life, liberty, or property, without due process of law; nor deny to any person within its jurisdiction the equal protection of the laws . . . ."

In addition to these constitutional sources, federal and state legislation may further refine and define the application of civil rights. Two important current examples of this are the legislative actions designed to improve educational opportunity for the handicapped and for women.

Since the application of legislation is sometimes not clearly understood, another source, the judiciary, attempts to ensure that the legislation is properly and fairly effected. Their interpretations and applications of the law may lead to a better understanding of the civil rights of students and teachers, but theirs is a record of inconsistent interpretation.

Finally, a blend of local custom, mores, and expectations, usually conservative, creates an unwritten code of behavior for students and teachers. This code is usually vague, imprecise, arbitrary, and seldom applied with consistency. Further, this source of restraint on civil rights may be applied at least as much to the private lives of students and teachers as to their school lives. This "code" can be as persistent as it is vague and should not be ignored.

2.2 STATUS OF TEACHER AND STUDENT RIGHTS

In October 1979 an athlete at a major college filed a lawsuit in excess of one million dollars against the coaching staff of the college, alleging harrassment following a poor punt. During the 1960s and 1970s it was frequently possible by reading the sports pages of the newspaper to follow part of the civil rights movement and observe coach/player conflicts over the player's right of symbolic expression. Students have been excluded from physical education clases for not having a "proper" uniform, for having long hair, and for doing many things that do not seem to be directly related to the conduct of the class. High school athletes have been excluded from participation for similar reasons, and also for such violations of school policy as getting married. Teachers and coaches are not free from criticism that seems to infringe upon their civil rights. They have been asked to refrain from wearing certain clothing, from keeping certain company, from refusing to take a certain oath—all of which today would probably be allowed by law, should one wish to follow that long and tortuous process.

It is important for one who is planning a career in physical education and sport to understand the present status of teacher and student rights and to prepare to follow legislated or adjudicated changes in that status. At the present time it is safe to say that the Constitution does not wait, "like a puppy waiting for his master, but instead it follows the student through the corridors, into the classroom, and onto the athletic field."[1] Yet while the constitutional rights of teachers and students seem guaranteed, there are exceptions.

2.3 PHYSICAL EDUCATION AND SPORT CASES

In 1972 a Montana high school student successfully brought legal action against his high school, which had ruled him ineligible for varsity football because he was married.[2] The student charged that the school board's policy toward married students would prohibit him from playing football in his last year of high school and therefore deprive him of the opportunity to obtain a college scholarship. The court supported the student.

The reappearance of long hair among high school students in the 1960s resulted in a number of violations of school and team dress codes and hair regulations. In some instances these regulations were challenged in court. While the results of the challenges were mixed, in at least one instance the court held that vague fears about possible damage to team discipline and team unity were insufficient to justify a hair rule for athletes.[3] In another instance the onus was placed on the coach to prove that long hair could interfere with athletic performance, and that without such proof there would be no more reason to accept hair regulations as a condition for playing on a team than for going to school.[4]

On the other side of the desk, a female physical education teacher was directed by the superintendent of schools and the high school principal to refrain from wearing a two-piece bathing suit while giving swimming instruction to junior high school boys. They alleged the suit was a distracting and disruptive influence. The teacher contested this directive, claiming that it "impinged upon her individual freedom." The New York Commissioner of Education ruled in the teacher's favor, stating the bathing suit was not disruptive of the educational process.[5] In a recent Texas case, a coach was dismissed because of his association with a local waitress. After a basketball game, the teacher and the waitress had parked on a country road and had been observed by a board member while doing so. The court ordered the teacher reinstated with back pay, awarded him attorney's fees, and said:

> School districts may examine the conduct of teachers both in and out of classrooms. . . . Nevertheless, before a teacher can possibly be discharged for personal conduct, the court feels that a showing must be made that such conduct had a direct effect on the teacher's success in performing classroom duties.[6]

These cases illustrate a current concern, that of protecting the constitutional rights of students and teachers. It it is quite appropriate to be concerned with this topic in physical education and sport. For years, perhaps ever since schools accepted extracurricular activities into their programs, some requirements were made of those students wishing to participate. Some of these requirements were stated as formal school policy, some as requirements for a particular team, club, or group. In some cases, these requirements may have infringed upon student rights. In many states, for example, the majority age has been lowered to eighteen, creating a delicate situation wherein students who legally can purchase and consume alcoholic beverages are prohibited from doing so by a team rule. Teachers have also suffered infringements on their individual freedom by restrictions on grooming, dress, selected subject matter, political activity, and many items too numerous to list. This discussion will focus on the rights of students as a guide for those who teach and coach them, and on the rights of those who teach and coach. Since many of the rights possessed by students and teachers vary from state to state and depend on state statutes and local board policy, the discussion focuses on those rights that tend to be consistent from state to state or that are assured by the Constitution of the United States. Teachers in their respective communities should refer to their state educational statutes, to stated policies of their local school board, and to their teacher's handbook for further clarification of their rights and responsibilities as teachers.

2.4 RIGHTS OF STUDENTS

Decisions pertaining to the rights of students fall into several categories, and in some of these categories it is possible to find evidence of decisions rendered that are relevant to coaches and physical educators. It appears that in the matter of basic student rights, physical educators and coaches need to be concerned about freedom of expression (including hair and dress), due process, corporal punishment, discrimination, school records, and grades and diplomas.[7]

2.5 FIRST AMENDMENT RIGHTS OF STUDENTS

School officials often try to justify their influence over student lives on the grounds that they are empowered to act *in loco parentis*. This term, which literally means "in the place of the parent," requires that an educator act as a parent would with respect to the care and supervision of a child and includes the power to discipline a child as a parent can. Courts are becoming skeptical of this argument and education officials are now finding limitations on their assumed authority. Two recent cases illustrate this point. The Ohio Department of Education rejected the idea that schools may act in place of the parent, and the New York State Board of Education took the position that educators have only the powers expressly granted to them by the legislature and that:

> The school and all its officers and employees stand in loco parentis only for the purpose of educating the child.[8]

These changes in the concept of *in loco parentis* have led to a reduction in the breadth and depth of regulation of student conduct. Rather than representing a blanket authority to regulate student behavior, rules and policies today should not penalize the student unless that student's behavior is directly related to the educational function of the school. In other words, any rules, policies, or regulations designed to control the behavior of students and student-athletes must be consistent with those rules, policies, and regulations that are necessary for the school to operate as an agent for education. While some inconsistencies, such as corporal punishment, do exist, the constitutional rights of a student are assured.

Children do have the right and usually the obligation to attend school for a certain number of years, usually about ten. This right and obligation has included, in theory, all children, but with the passage of Public Law 94-142, the Education of All Handicapped Act, those with mental or physical handicaps have had their opportunity for a "regular" education enhanced. This act provides the right to a free, public education and in many cases limits the charging of fees to students. In Michigan, for example, fees may not be charged for anything that is an integral, fundamental part of the elementary and secondary education. Michigan includes interscholastic athletics in this category, along with books, school supplies, and equipment.[9]

There have been numerous challenges by students to attempts by school authorities to control their behavior. Many of these challenges were directed at restrictions of the First Amendment guarantees of freedom of expression. In 1969, the United States Supreme Court held that students do not lose their right to free expression under the First Amendment to the Constitution when they enter school. In a significant decision in *Tinker* v. *Des Moines Independent School District*, the courts said the students may be prevented from expressing their views only when they "materially and substantially" disrupt the work and discipline of the school.[10] The Tinker decision (commonly called the Tinker test) is a clear-cut statement, applicable to all schools, of a student's right to constitutional guarantees in the school. The "material and substantial disruption" is the essence of the Tinker test. This test should be the starting point in considering regulations which may restrict student behavior guaranteed by the First Amendment. Since the term "material and substantial" has no strict definition, the Tinker test requires the physical educator or coach to be judicious in the use of restrictive rules and policies as, for example, in dress and hair codes.

These two issues received a great deal of publicity (perhaps more than they warranted) in the late 1960s and early 1970s. Standards for both dress and hair length were regulated by school officials, including teachers and coaches. Under the Tinker test, unless coaches can show that long hair interferes with athletic performance, there is now no reason for regulating hair length as a condition for playing on a team than as a condition for going to school. If hair length can constitutionally be regulated as a requirement for school attendance, it may be regulated for athletic participation; but in those states which to not permit the regulation of hair for attendance, hair length may not be regulated for athletics unless the Tinker test is successfully applied. As to dress, wherever hair length can be regulated, dress can be regulated as long as the regulations are reasonable and do not infringe upon free expression, including symbolic expression.

While dress may or may not be regulated the right to a free public education prohibits requiring students to purchase a particular gym uniform, but does allow a school to require students to wear appropriate clothes that enable them to perform the activities of the class.

2.6 DUE PROCESS RIGHTS OF STUDENTS

School authorities frequently find, of course, that it is necessary to enforce discipline. In doing so they have shown little, if any, desire to go through the rigorous procedures of a trial, but at the other extreme, they have at times taken a remarkably lax approach to ensure fairness. The right to due process is the right to be treated fairly, not be deprived of life, liberty, or property, and not be punished for alleged misconduct without first having certain established procedures followed in assessing one's innocence or guilt. Occasionally, due process is violated in physical education and athletics. This usually occurs in cases of suspension from an athletic team. Students are entitled to know what they are accused of and should be given the chance to tell their side of the story. This presupposes that they knew what was expected of them. In addition to ensuring due process, these minimal procedures would promote understanding and empathy and encourage effective student-teacher communication.

The right to due process also means that any punishment imposed must be in proportion to the offense committed. Since courts are recognizing that extracurricular activities are a fundamental part of the school's educational program, any denial of the opportunity to participate in these activities can be as serious as suspension from school. Any suspension of this sort should, therefore, involve due process. As the United States Supreme Court held in the landmark due process case of *Goss v Lopez*:

> A student's legitimate entitlement to a public education is a property interest which is protected by the Due Process Clause. . . . Where a person's good name, reputation, honor or integrity is at stake because of what the government is doing to him, the minimal requirements of the Clause must be satisfied.[11]

The essential point for teachers and coaches to remember is fairness. Be sure that students are given the opportunity to know what is expected of them, that they are informed precisely of what they allegedly did that was wrong, and that they are given a chance to relate their version of the incident.

2.7 CORPORAL PUNISHMENT

The use of physical force to punish students is certainly not new. At one time it was not regarded as a teacher's last resort, but as the "first resort and true remedy." Corporal punishment was the cornerstone of school discipline. Kelly relates the following scene:

> A new teacher seized a long rod by both ends, and lifting it high over his head, said fiercely, as his first words to his class: "do you see that rod? Would you like to feel it? If you would, just break any of the 49 rules I'm going to read to you."[12]

Flogging became such a part of school routine that in one Massachusetts school of 250 students there were 328 floggings in one week, or an average of more than 65 each day.

The use of corporal punishment by school authorities is permissible under certain guidelines. It should be remember, however, that the use of *excessive* physical force by school authorities on students is illegal. The use of physical force on students should, of course, be a last resort, but in those rare instances when corporal punishment is deemed necessary, it should adhere to guidelines for the use of such punishment. In Montana, for example, corporal punishment must be administered in the presence of another teacher or principal, and with notice given to a parent or guardian, except in cases of open defiance, when no notice is required.[13] Many other states have guidelines for administering corporal punishment; some, such as Massachusetts and New Jersey, have laws forbidding all corporal punishment in schools.

Even though corporal punishment is permitted in schools, it is not advocated. The National Education Association has recommended the immediate abolition of "infliction of physical pain upon students" for purposes of discipline.[14] Their argument is abetted by the fact that corporal punishment has been prohibited for many years in the military services and, more recently, in prisons as well. If corporal punishment is used, it must meet the guidelines of your state, must not be a first-line punishment for misbehavior, and generally must take place only in the presence of a second school official who must be informed beforehand and in the student's presence of the reason for the punishment. The punishment must not be unreasonable, unnecessary, or excessive. Both state and federal courts have held that a student can sue a teacher who injures him or her in the course of administering corporal punishment. The terms *unreasonable, unnecessary, excessive,* among others, do not lend themselves well to precise definition, and this compels any teacher or coach who uses physical force on a student to do so judiciously.

This was the case in Louisiana in 1967, when the parents of a student injured as a result of disciplinary action were awarded $2,500.[15] The fourteen-year-old boy, 4 feet 9 inches tall and weighing 101 pounds, was a student in a physical education class. The teacher was 34 years old, 5 feet 8 inches tall, and weighed 230 pounds. The student readily conceded that he was behaving contrary to the order of the teacher and was ordered off the basketball court while the rest of the class was learning how to shoot lay-ups. The student reentered the basketball court and was again ordered to the sidelines. The student again reentered the court and the teacher decided discipline was required.

The student and the teacher presented irreconcilable versions of what followed. The teacher stated that the student tried to strike him and he grasped the boy's arm to restrain him., The student struggled to get free, fell to the floor, and injured his arm. The student, on the other hand, alleged that the teacher menaced and chased him around the court, grabbed him, lifted him from the ground, shook him against the folded bleachers, and released him suddenly so that he fell to the floor and fractured his arm.

The court found its credulity taxed to believe that the teacher's physical safety was threatened by a blow from the student. The court held that simple restraint by the teacher would have been sufficient. It ruled that the teacher's actions in lifting, shaking, and dropping the student were clearly in excess of the physical force necessary to either discipline the student or to protect himself, and that this lack of judgment on the part of the teacher subjected the defendants (the teachers and the Parish School Board) to liability for the injuries.

2.8 OTHER STUDENT RIGHTS

There are other categories of rights of students which occasionally concern a teacher or coach. These are discrimination, school records, grades and diplomas, and search and seizure.

Discrimination

In school, students have the right not to be discriminated against on the basis of race, religion, ethnic background, sex, or handicap. It is the last two categories that today are of most immediate concern to physical educators and coaches as they attempt to fulfill the intent of Title IX of the Education Amendments Act of 1972, and the Education for All Handicapped Act, commonly called Public Law or P.L. 94-142. More explicit guidelines for fulfilling the requirements of these laws will be given in a later chapter.

School Records

School records are included because many teachers and coaches do not realize for what length of time student records, particularly those concerned with accident or injury, need to be stored. If you are teaching elementary, junior high, or high school students, nearly all of the students will be minors, under the age at which they have full legal rights and duties, including the right to sue. Depending on state regulations, a student may bring suit for an injury suffered as a minor up to two or three years after he or she reaches majority age, the age at which full legal rights and duties are assumed.[16] Thus, an eight-year-old injured in a physical education calss may be able to seek recourse for those injuries at the age of majority, and the appropriate records may then be necessary.

Grades and Diplomas

The question of denying a student a diploma because he or she failed physical education has arisen, and despite the fact that most states require some physical education, the law pertaining to the question is unclear. In New York, the State Commissioner of Education has ruled that a local board of education may *not* refuse graduation or promotion because of failure in physical education.[17] The Commissioner has also held that a local board may not ignore the refusal of a student to participate in physical education throughout the school year and deny the student graduation or advancement without warning. Some advance notice stating the maximum number of permissible absences and a warning of the possibility of not graduating is required.

Search and Seizure

School property is state property, and even though schools often supply lockers to students, the state or its agency retains control of them. At this writing, courts have not required that in the search of student lockers students must first give consent. A different situation exists with the search of an individual student and his own property. In the search of a student's person, for example, it is usually a good policy to refrain from actually coming into contact with the student but instead to direct that he empty his pockets or other personal effects. That strategy, in effect, constitutes student consent. Courts have been consistent in upholding searches of student lockers and even student vehicles while on school property. Courts are not in complete agreement about the search of a student's person, but searches have been upheld where probable cause existed.

2.9 PERMISSIBLE LIMITS ON PARTICIPATION
IN EXTRACURRICULAR ACTIVITIES

The discussion thus far indicates that students do retain their constitutional rights when they attend school and that these rights are to be assured in athletic programs and other extracurricular events. Some regulation, however, is necessary and allowed. In general, courts allow schools great leeway in formulating rules and will not interfere with the regulation of extracurricular activities unless they are arbitrary, unreasonable, or capricious. The courts appear to be reluctant to overrule school officials, so long as the officials act in good faith. The following limits on participation seem acceptable, according to a September 1978 legal memorandum on the "Regulation of Student Participation in Extracurricular Activities" published by the National Association of Secondary School Principals.[18]

1. School officials or the associations to which they have delegated their authority can make reasonable rules excluding students with physical disabilities from extracurricular activities. These rules must be reasonably calculated to protect the student from harm and the school from liability. The American Medical Association has advised that students be disqualified from contact sports if they are without one of two organs such as an eye or a kidney. Cases involving students with prosthetic devices have not been decided with consistency.

2. A school may ban a pregnant student from certain types of extracurricular activities because of the potential dangers involved. A school may not discriminate on the basis of a student's false pregnancy, termination of pregnancy, or recovery therefrom. In such cases, the school can require a doctor's certificate of the student's physical and emotional readiness to participate if it requires such certification from other students with conditions requiring medical attention.

3. Participation in extracurricular activities may be limited by reasonable rules relating to a student's age. Such rules are generally upheld as necessary for the safety of participants and to equalize competitive conditions.

4. General "transfer" rules that provide that a student who transfers from one school district to another without a change in residency by a parent or guardian is ineligible to participate in extracurricular activities for one year have generally been upheld by the courts. One recognized exception is when students are required to transfer by law, as in desegregation "busing" situations.

5. The authority of school officials to make reasonable rules relating to school attendance as a condition of participating extracurricular activities has not been seriously challenged.

6. Schools and state associations have the authority to regulate participation in extracurricular activities on the basis of a student's conduct in or out of school, so long as the student's conduct is controlled by written codes that detail prohibited conduct and contain fair and reasonable penalities for violations.

2.10 RIGHTS OF TEACHERS

One would hardly think that a discussion of the rights of teachers would be necessary. After all, do not teachers have the same rights as others? Historically, the answer is a qualified no. Teachers have traditionally been held to a higher standard of conduct than have other public employees and professionals, a state at least partially attributable to the religious roots of American education. Moreover, this higher standard of conduct has caused direct controls to be placed on the private lives of teachers.

Today, one occasionally will read of a teacher/administrator clash over a personal habit or lifestyle deemed inappropriate for a community. One need not go back too many years to recall instances of harrassment of teachers because of beards, long hair, and clothing — the "counterculture" appearance. Physical education teachers have been threatened with loss of their job because of severe obesity and the poor "role model" they presented to their students. Many teachers have been privately and publicly chastized because of their cohabitation arrangements. Many beginning teachers have found that the cultural shock they experienced upon leaving home and entering a more liberal university environment was small compared to the cultural shock they encountered when they left the academic milieu and returned to a smaller, more conservative community. It has not bee uncommon to find teachers with nearly as many restrictions on their private behavior as students, particularly new teachers during their probationary period.

However, the concept of teachers' rights has been liberalized. In recent years, the federal constitution has emerged as a significant source of teachers' rights. Increasingly, the courts are affording protection to teachers on the basis of the First Amendment to the

Constitution and the due process and equal protection clauses of the Fourteenth Amendment. The Constitution is supplemented by other sources of teachers' rights, such as state constitutional provisions, state and federal statutes, policies of state and local boards of education, collective bargaining agreements, and in individual contracts.[16]

2.11 ACADEMIC FREEDOM AND FREE SPEECH

In general, a teacher may not be dismissed because he or she has exercised a right protected by the United States Constiution. After reviewing decisions pertaining to teachers' rights one is able to come to a conclusion similar to that of the Tinker Test of students' rights, that is, the behavior of the teacher, of and by itself, is not sufficient cause for dismissal. There must be a "material and substantial" disruption in the educational function of the school as a result of the teacher's behavior in order for that behavior to be prohibited. A topic frequently examined under this test is that of academic freedom. A teacher is guaranteed a significant amount of academic freedom. This academic freedom, however, is modified and restricted by the school's right to prescribe the general subject matter to be discussed by the teacher. Academic freedom does not grant teachers a license to say or write whatever they choose, but rather "the propriety of regulations or sanctions must depend on such circumstances as the age and sophistication of the students, the closeness of the relation between the specific technique used and some concededly valid education objective and the context and manner of presentation."[20]

A teacher's methods are not without limits, but the limits have been quite broad. As an example, the Atlanta Board of Education refused to reinstate a former junior high school coach who was fired for telling his team to "kill" the opposition.[21] The scouting report distributed by this coach stated: "All of the coaches hate them and their coaches and if you're going to beat them Saturday, you'll have to hate them also. So much that when we mean kill, we mean to the death."

The American concept of academic freedom includes the right of teachers to express themselves freely in their private capacities without reprisals by school or government authorities. This includes political expression, including participation in demonstrations. A teacher may, however, forfeit his constitutional protection if he or she exceeds the legitimate bounds of criticism and protest sheltered by the First Amendment. One court, for example, found that a teacher who stooped to name calling and personal invective in statements about his administrative supervisor and staff and who challenged the integrity of the school board's administrative staff was not sheltered by the Constitution from the consequences of his acts, and that the board's refusal to renew his contract because of such staements did not violate his right to free speech.[22] Other rights associated with free speech guaranteed to teachers include the right to run for public office (although the teacher may have to take a leave of absence while campaigning), to join a union, to support a strike, and to associate with persons holding unconventional social views. No longer may a teacher be required to take a "loyalty" oath,, unless that oath is properly limited, as an oath to "Uphold the Constitution of the United States and of the State . . . and . . . faithfully perform the duties of the position upon which he is about to enter."[23]

2.12 FREEDOM IN PRIVATE LIFE

A teacher's private conduct, standing alone, cannot constitutionally be cause for dismissal. There again is a sort of Tinker test that forces the state or the school authorities to show that the teacher's conduct has impaired his or her fitness to teach. There must be some "ascertainable deleterious effect on the efficiency of the service."[24] One exception to this is the occasionally upheld requirement that a teacher live within the boundaries of the employing jurisdiction. School authorities cannot constitutionally discipline or terminate the employment of a teacher because that teacher does not conform to conventional standards of grooming or personal appearance. Exceptions exist, particularly in the case of physical education teachers who are severely overweight. For the most part restrictions on dress and grooming have been regarded as infringements upon the "symbolic speech" assured citizens in the First and Fourteenth Amendments and as invasions of privacy. Similarly, teachers are assured freedom of religion, and these assurances are applicable to agnostics and atheists.[25] Teachers should not be discriminated against on the basis of race, sex, or age, but in these days of alleged discrimination and alleged reverse discrimination, guidelines are hard to find. Finally, supporting all of the aforementioned rights, teachers do have the constitutional protection of procedural rights, including due process.

2.13 TENURE

One of the unique rights of a teacher is tenure — the possession of an automatically renewable contract unless there is a material breach of the contract on the part of the teacher. While tenure has been under attack by school boards, administrators, and legislators, it is still the rule rather than the exception. The essential provisions of a tenure contract are that the teacher's contract is automatically renewable, normally after serving a certain number or years called a probationary period, and that dismissals thereafter may be made only for specific causes which must be established by timely notice and opportunity to be heard thereon before dismissal.[26] Some of the specific causes for dismissal are incompetence, insubordination, immorality or immoral conduct, neglect of duty, and refusal to obey the orders of superiors. While tenure is by no means universal, and the rigors of the probationary period are not exactly the same from state to state or even from school district to school district, tenure is a commonly found contractual professional right of teachers.

2.14 THE TEN COMMANDMENTS FOR TEACHERS

In the June 1979 issue of *Phi Delta Kappan*, Thomas R. McDaniel presents a guide for teachers in the form of "shall nots" designed to keep educators out of trouble in an age of litigation.[27]

   I. Thou shalt not worship in the classroom.
  II. Thou shalt not abuse academic freedom.
 III. Thou shalt not engage in private activities that impair teaching effectiveness.
  IV. Thou shalt not deny students due process.
   V. Thou shalt not punish behavior through academic penalities.
  VI. Thou shalt not misuse corporal punishment.
 VII. Thou shalt not neglect students' safety.
VIII. Thou shalt not slander or libel your students.
  IX. Thou shalt not photocopy in violation of the copyright law.
   X. Thou shalt not be ignorant of the law.

These commandments are not written in stone, but they do seem to summarize accurately the professional rights and responsibilities of teachers at present. Each of the commandments has many implications, and an understanding of these provides a guide for the behavior of teachers and coaches.

NOTES

1. *Dunham* v. *Pulsifer*, 312 F. Supp. 411 (D. Vt. 1970).
2. *Moran* v. *School District #7. Yellowstone County.* 350 F. Supp. 1180 (D. Mont. 1972).
3. *Dunham* v. *Pulsifer.*
4. *Long* v. *Zopp*, 476 F.2d 180 (4th Cir. 1973).
5. In the Matter of Heather Martin, No. 8156 (N.Y. Commissioner of Education) August 3, 1971. Cited in : David Rubin, *The Rights of Teachers* (New York: Avon Books, 1968), pp. 119-120.
6. *Coddell* v. *Johnson,* Civil Action No. Ca-7-615 (N.D. Tex. June 30, 1972). Cited in Rubin, *The Rights of Teachers,* pp. 11-112.
7. Alan Levine and Eve Cary, *The Rights of Students* (New York: Avon Books, 1973), p. 12.
8. Ibid., p. 13.
9. Ibid., pp. 20-21.
10. *Tinker* v. *Des Moines School District.* 393 U.S. 503 (1969).
11. *Goss* v. *Lopez,* 419 U.S. 565 (1975).
12. Cynthia Kelly, "Spare the Road and . . . " *Update.* American Bar Association Fall 1977, pp.16-17.
13. Section 20-4-302, *Montana Code Annotated.* 1978.
14. Levine and Cary, *The Rights of Students.* p. 83.
15. *Frank* v. *Orleans Parish School Board,* 195 So.2d. 451 (La. App. 1967).
16. Betty van der Smissen, "Consideration of Legal Implications for Sponsoring Agencies and Activity Leaders of Adventure Recreation Programs" (Lecture delivered at the American Association for Leisure and Recreation Session on Legal Aspects of Risk Recreation, AAHPER National Convention, Kansas City, Mo., April 8, 1978.
17. Levine and Cary, *The Rights of Students.* p. 118.
18. "Regulation of Student Participation in Extracurricular Activities. A Legal Memorandum of the National Association of Secondary School Principals, Reston, Va., September 1978.
19. David Rubin, *The Rights of Teachers* (New York: Avon Books, 1968).
20. *Mailloux* v *Kiley.* 323 F. Supp. 1387 (D. Mass. 1971), aff'd 448 F.2d 1242. (1st Cir. 1971).
21. Reported in the *Los Angeles Times.* September 17, 1976.
22. *Jones* v. *Battles,* 315 F. Supp. 601 (D. Conn. 1970).
23. *Rubin,* The Rights of Teachers, pp. 48-104.
24. Ibid. p. 108.
25. Ibid., p. 106.
26. Ibid., p. 152.
27. Thomas McDaniel, "The Teacher's Ten Commandments: School Law in the Classroom," *Phi Delta Kappan.* June 1979, pp. 703-708.

3

SAFE ENVIRONMENT FOR PHYSICAL EDUCATION AND SPORT ACTIVITIES

3.1 INTRODUCTION

Most lawsuits in physical education and sport contain an allegation of an unsafe or hazardous area or facility. This is not surprising, as even a cursory examination of a playing field or gymnasium may reveal a feature that could become a factor in an injury. This is especially true of old gymnasia and multipurpose gymnasia.

Some hazards are more apparent than others. For high school games, a small school in South Dakota used a floor which on one end had a stage that extended out as far as the basket and on the other end a stairway that extended into the right forecourt. On one end a player drove to the basket with caution; on the other end, ten players were crowded on one side of an already small floor. In another case, a Minnesota football field was once lined with unslaked lime.[1] During the course of play, an athlete was thrown to the ground and his face was forced into the lime. As a result, he lost the sight of one eye and seriously impaired the sight of the other.

In some cases, the hazardous condition may not be noticed for a number of years. In one such instance, a community recreation program used a combination cafeteria, assembly, and gymnasium for an adult basketball program.[2] During play in this program, a thirty-year-old man went up for a shot near the basket. His momentum carried him beyond the end line into a door behind the basket. He tried to brace himself against the door, but in so doing his arm went through a panel made of ordinary window glass. Action was successfully taken against the school district because the glass was not shatterproof or reinforced, and there were no warnings indicating this. The jury held for the plaintiff despite testimony by the building's architect that shatterproof glass panels were not necessary, despite fifteen years of safe use of the area for basketball, and despite testimony by the custodian that during that time the glass panels in the door were never broken.

Lawsuits involving athletic areas, facilities, and equipment were even isolated for special attention by the Washington State Legislature in limiting the application of sovereign immunity.[3] The statute reads:

> No action shall be brought or maintained against any school district or its officers for any noncontractual acts or omission of such district, its agents, officers or employees, relating to any park, playground, or field house, athletic apparatus or appliance, or manual training equipment, whether situated in or about any school house or elsewhere, owned, operated or maintained by such school district (RCWA 28.58.030).

This statute was interpreted by the Washington courts to mean that a school district was exempt from liability only in the case of injuries resulting from the negligence of its agents in relation to athletic apparatus on or in an area used for physical activity by the school, and not from injury sustained as a result of negligent supervision of activities or students. This statute was later amended to remove any immunity (RCWA 28A.58.020).

It is essential that anyone teaching or coaching a physical activity be adept at examining an area or facility to ensure that the activity can be safely conducted on or in that environment. Court cases alleging unsafe conditions are present in all sports, and every professional needs to develop a critical eye to detect unsafe conditions. This implies foreseeability. A teacher or coach must be aware of the inherent danger in the activity, of possible injuries resulting from the activity, and with this in mind examine the facility to be used. The goal is to eliminate the likelihood of injury due to a risk not present in the activity.

3.2 SAFE PREMISES

Schools are not ensurers of safety, but schools must provide a safe environment for education. The essence of this duty is that schools must provide and maintain facilities relatively free from injury producing conditions. This does not imply that all risk is eliminated. It does mean that risks, especially those risks not an inherent part of an activity, are not to be created because of the nature of the facility.

The people who have most of the responsibility for providing safe premises are those in immediate supervision of the area. As part of their general supervisory duties, some of the responsibility will fall to the school principal, some to the athletic director, and some to the department chairperson. More will fall to the teacher in immediate control of the area. Part of any teacher's duties is to regularly and thoroughly inspect the area, warn the students of any hazards, especially any hidden or changed hazards, and make written recommendations to their superiors that such hazards or defects be remedied.

3.3 SAFE PREMISES DUTIES

How regular and thorough does the inspection need to be? Unfortunately, there are few guidelines available because the question because cyclical—these inspections should be regular and thorough enough to discover hazards, but if a hazard is not discovered then the inspection is not adequate. In one example involving playground equipment, school officials testified that the playground slide had been inspected just prior to an accident.[4] They also indicated that the slide appreared in the same condition both before and after the injury, with some screws missing from crosspieces under the bottom of the slide. The court felt that while these inspections were regular enough, they were not thorough enough in that the potential danger of the missing screws was overlooked. Teachers and coaches are responsible for fixing those conditions that are observed (actual notice), and for those conditions that are not observed but should have been observed (constructive notice).

It is also necesary to warn students of any risks, including those risks presented by the facility or area. According to the standard of care presently at use, such a warning must ensure not only that the students are aware of the danger and the risk, but that they know, understand, and appreciate the danger and the risks involved. In other words, teachers should take great care, and probably more time than they want in explaining and emphasizing the potential risks not only of a certain sport but also of that sport played in that particular area. It is a good idea to have warnings of this sort in written form placed in such a location (as the inside cover of a play book or the door of the student's locker) that the students will constantly have this notice in front of them.

The third duty of a teacher or coach in providing safe premises is to inform his or her superiors of the hazard and the risk created and request that the hazard be eliminated as quickly as possible. This notice and request should also be in writing and addressed to whomever may be concerned. It probably would not always be expected of a teacher or coach to take hammer and nail in hand to immediately repair or remove a hazardous condition. It is expected that a teacher or coach because of proximity to the area and expertise in the subject be able to see that which needs to be changed and inform his or her superiors. If one does this, and one persists in efforts to have the hazard repaired or removed, the onus is transferred to one's superiors.

It is important to recall again the standard of care which applies to a teacher or coach—that of a reasonably prudent professional. Thus in ensuring that you and your students are in a safe place, this place is one regarded as safe by a reasonably prudent teacher or coach.

3.4 EXAMPLES OF ALLEGED UNSAFE PREMISES

In a New York case, a playground was used for a number of purposes, including ice skating and softball.[5] The field was constructed so that the floor was cemented and a two-inch curbing above the floor extended around the entire field separating the field from the pedestrian walk. Upon the pedestrian walk and near the curb were several concrete benches. A twenty-five-year-old man who played softball on the diamond on Sundays attempted to catch the ball, tripped upon the curb, fell and struck a concrete bench, sustaining a serious injury. The plaintiff claimed that the playground was negligently designed and constructed for the purpose of playing softball games, and that it was a dangerous and unsafe place for the playing of such games. In decided for the defendant, the court held that the young man's age and prior playing experience on the field indicated a voluntary and knowing exposure to the risk involved, and he so assumed those risks.

In another case a seemingly minor point resulted in victory for the plaintiff because of an unsafe environment for an activity. In this case, the plaintiff was playing with an outdoor, rubber-tipped, badminton shuttlecock.[6] He and his companion were playing in a poorly lighted basement room used as a boiler room, for equipment and storage, and for crafts. For three weeks the room was used as an area for batting the shuttlecock back and forth. A playground leader was present, but had never stopped the activity. The plaintiff asserted that the defendant (in this case, the City of Reading) owed a duty to children to provide reasonably safe conditions. The poor lighting was found to be the proximate cause of injury, and poor lighting to be a negligent act of the city. In commenting on the case, the court said:

> The place in which they were playing obviously was hazardous for such activity, by reason of the poor lighting conditions, and of the restricted space available (which was but a fraction of the size of a regulation badminton court). The result of their inability to move freely about was that each player attempted to hit the shuttlecock directly toward his opponent rather than away from him as in a normal badminton game. The manner in which minor plaintiff and Richard were playing was also dangerous. The close proximity of the children to each other, the use of an outdoor shuttlecock with a hard rubber-tip, instead of an indoor one with a cork tip in the still air of this room, and the absence of a badminton net, all were circumstances which helped create a

dangerous situation. . . . All these facts and circumstances, when considered together, show clearly that these children were allowed to continue playing in a situation of obvious danger.[6]

3.5 GENERAL CONSIDERATIONS

In the cases cited, the defendant was a city or school district and not a teacher or coach, but a teacher or coach may well be charged with negligence, or listed as a co-defendant if he allows a dangerous condition to occur or persist. A supervisor, whether engaged in general or specific supervision, plays a key role in providing and maintaining a safe environment by carrying out the three duties listed herein to the standard of care of a reasonable and prudent professional. By carrying out these duties teachers and students should see the following results in their programs:

1. A recognition and understanding of the hazards of all activities and facilities;
2. the removal of all unnecessary hazards of facilities, equipment, and programming;
3. compensation through education and protective equipoment for those hazards that cannot be removed;
4. creation of no new hazards.[7]

All apparatus and facilities should be inspected and tested thoroughly before the opening of school or the season of its use. In addition, inspections should be made at the end of the season of use so that repairs and replacements can be made before the equipment is to be reused. To facilitate these inspections, a checklist as shown in Figure 3-1 may be valuable for organizing one's inspection of a facility and the equipment.

Fig. 3.1

Safety Checklist

Health and Physical Education Department

Semiannual Inspection_____
                                    (date)

Made By: _____

Custodian: _____

General Safe Practices

No.	Item	Yes	No

1. Are facilities checked by the custodian-engineer and the director or equipment and facility manager for safety at least twice each year? _____

2. Do instructors check equipment and facilities before each usage? _____

3. Is there an established system of writing to the proper authority to report needed repairs to facilities? _____

4. Is apparatus put away, locked, roped off, or covered with mats when not in use under supervisor? _____

5. Are any activities conducted for which adequate protective equipment cannot be furnished? _____

6. Are intramural and physical education class participants furnished the same adequate protective equipment as the varsity? _____

7. Is there an established method of accident reporting and follow-up? _____

8. Is there an established policy of rendering first aid and treating injuries received in physical education classes, intramurals, and athletics?

9. Is there an established policy of notifying parents regarding transportation and hospitalization of injured pupils? _____

10. Are the students taking physical education and participating in intramurals covered in the athletic benefit plan? _____

11. Are pupils assigned to activities or permitted to play on teams on the basis of health examinations, tests, and ability? _____

12. Are any classes or activities overcrowded for facilities available? _____

13. Are passage facilities safe and is there a safe system of pedestrian traffic within the athletic plant? _____

14. Are doors locked at any time in violation of fire ordinances? _____

15. Is the number of spectators that is safe for each area determined and the limit strictly adhered to? _____

16. Are there adequate fire extinguishers in every area, and are all staff members trained in the methods of correct operation?   _____

17. Are students trained in the proper fire-drill procedures for all areas and activities of the department?   _____

Reprinted by permission from Don C. Seaton, Herbert J. Stack, and Bernard Loft, *Administration and Supervision of Safety Education* (New York: Macmillan, 1969), pp. 254-258.

3.6 SPORT SPECIFICITY

In addition to these general considerations, regular and thorough inspections must be made of the areas in which certain activities occur. No two activities have exactly the same risks. Every sport has inherent risks, but these risks differ not only among sports but also within a sport if it is taught in different areas or to different grades or skill levels. The potential risk in indoor touch football is somewhat different from the potential risk in outdoor touch football. There are certain injuries that are likely to occur in a certain sport; there are certain injuries that are likely to occur in certain locations in certain sports. For example, in racquetball there is a potential for eye injuries, and the potential is so great that eyeguards should be worn by players. In addition, most eye injuries occur near the center court area when the player at center court is watching the opponent strike the ball in the back court. A teacher or coach would, of course, warn students of this hazard in the sport, but because the tendency in most sports is to emphasize watching the ball, the risk of injury is high and needs to be reduced through the use of eyeguards. It was not always so. The first thorough instructional book on racquetball includes a picture of two professionals playing. The player in back is about to hit a kill shot; the player in front is watching without the use of eyeguards. The caption for the picture suggests that better players always keep their eye on the ball.[8] This suggests the student do the same. The teacher, however, should tell the students the book is incorrect and should re-emphasize the potential severity of eye injuries in the sport.

The point is that risks and hazards tend to be specific to certain activities. Within a given sport there are certain risks likely to occur in certain situations. One who teaches that sport must become aware of these sport-specific injuries and hazardous conditions and thus reduce the likelihood of injury. It is important that teachers and coaches develop skills in both general safety and education and in safety education for the sports they teach. It is also important for teachers and coaches to have access to injury-reporting systems, to current information regarding teaching specific sports, and to information about the results of lawsuits in their specific sports, because legal rulings tend to become operational guidelines. This information is available in safety education texts, from magazines and journals devoted to specific sports, and from texts that review and summarize cases in specific sports, such as *Legal Liability of Cities and Schools for Injuries in Recreation and Parks*, by Betty Van der Smissen.[9] It is all a part of one's continuing professional preparation.

3.7 UNSAFE AREAS

What is an unsafe area? The answer, unfortunately, is usually discovered *ex post facto*. Just as the law is a bit inconsistent when applied to sport, the concept of safe place is subject to variation, depending on the particular circumstances of a case. The next section of this chapter is designed to acquaint you with some of the conditions which have been alleged to be unsafe in a few sports. This section is not meant to be exhaustive but instead representative of things to look for while inspecting an activity area for a specific sport.

Unsafe Areas in Specific Sports

Baseball/Softball. Unsafe conditions have been alleged because of curbs around the diamond, poor design and layout so that fields overlap, inadequate bleachers, inadequate or poorly repaired screens, inadequate barriers between playing fields and nearby traffic, conditions of playing field, apparatus for other sports left on the field, nearby incinerators, inadequate fences, bases and items used as bases, and spikes to hold bases in place.

Basketball. Unsafe conditions have been alleged because of contiguous courts placed too close, walls and door jambs too near the basket and inadequately padded, windows behind baskets without unbreakable glass, movable backstops, too small an area, unpadded basketball goal posts, multiple use of a gymnasium, inadequate bleachers, spectators too close to the floor, and slippery floor.

Football. Unsafe conditions have been alleged because of the use of unslaked lime to line the field, adjacent equipment, nearby traffic, improperly supported equipment (tackling dummies), inadequate bleachers, lack of proper first aid equipment on premises, condition of playing field, sideline markers too close and not properly manned, lack of protective padding on surfaces near the playing area, spectators too close to playing area.

Track and Field. Unsafe conditions have been alleged primarily in connection with throwing events, in which the throwing area was either improperly laid out or allowed traffic to pass too close to the throwing area. Other track and field cases involve poor design of pole vault standards and placement of pole vault box; and presence of other activities too close to the track and field area.

Aquatics. Unsafe conditions have been alleged because of the use of shallow pools, inadequate number and placement of lifeguards, handrails and stairways unsafe, collapsing bathhouses, inadequate lighting, slippery surfaces, objects in the water, murky water, sewer overflow, inadequate barriers between swimming and nonswimming areas, and inadequate warning signs. In addition, some unusual instances have occurred, the most memorable being a situation in which the pool was located near a bear's den. In another case, plaintiff brought lawsuit following an injury suffered because of inadequately marked depth markers. Although the depth markers were clearly marked with a number, the plaintiff was from a country that uses the metric system and assumed the depth of the water indicated was in meters and not in feet.[10]

Golf. Unsafe conditions have been alleged in golf with the design and layout of the course, especially when fairways adjoin; putting a golf course in too small an area; traffic, both vehicular and pedestrian; defective bridges; presence of a cement abutment in a clubhouse hallway with inadequate light; slippery and dangerous conditions of the floor; and three-wheeled golf carts.

Gymnastics and Playground Activities. Unsafe conditions have been alleged involving the horizontal bar; high bar; chinning bar; side horse; spring board; ladders; jungle gym; monkey bars; trapeze; balance beam; inadequate number and location of spotters; improperly placed mats; defective apparatus; defective supports for apparatus; installation of apparatus, particularly with placing horizontal ladders too high; slippery floor; and improper equipment allowed on the playground.

3.8 RECOMMENDATIONS

Since so many of the lawsuits in physical education and sport activities involve an allegation of an unsafe area or facility, and since so many of the present facilities were not designed for the varied activities of present-day sport and physical education programs, the professional who teaches or coaches should endeavor to provide a facility for the activity as free from hazardous conditions as possible. If one is fortunate enough to take part in the planning of facilities it is imperative that recommendations and standards such as those found in *Planning Facilities for Athletics, Physical Education, and Recreation* be followed.[11] In some cases, it may be necessary to go beyond the general recommendations in such books and refer to other books and articles that develop more detailed and more precise standards for specific activities. In addition to these sources, the following guidelines are suggested.

Inspection

All facilities should be inspected and tested before the opening of a season or semester. This inspection should be thorough and should continue on a regular basis, appropriate to the activity. The facility, apparatus, and equipment used by an instructor should be observed each day it is used, with specific problem points inspected at least weekly, or more often if appropriate.

Playing Surfaces

All playing surfaces, except those specialized surfaces for such activities as golf and cross-country, should be level, smooth, free from potentially harmful materials, and of proper texture for the activity. According to Seaton, a good playing surface should have resilience, good drainage, durability, nonabrasiveness, cleanliness, firmness, smoothness, general utility, good appearance, be free from dust, and be procurable at a reasonable cost.[12] Constant care must be taken to keep the play areas free from potentially harmful extraneous material, as well as from holes, bumps, and uneven sufaces. Indoor surfaces are free of some of these problems but are frequently slippery. All playing surfaces should avoid surrounding or overhanging obstructions that may cause injury. Sufficient space must be provided for play, with barriers and padding used wherever necessary to prevent an overlap of teaching areas and to prevent injury caused by running into an unpadded object. Most sports require that play areas be defined by lines. These are there, in part, for safety purposes, and the lines should be neither omitted nor allowed to become indistinct. If tape is used for lines, it must be examined periodically so that it remains tight to the floor. The area surrounding a play area should be examined daily so that extraneous objects do not become hazards. Adequate lighting is essential. Bleachers should not be accessible for play, and should be put up, taken down, or moved only by reliable workers. Doors should not open into play areas, should have recessed handles, and should never be locked during activity periods. For all areas, emergency exits should be visible and unobstructed. Emergency procedures should be posted, be clear, and be emphasized.

On the playing area, movable equipment and apparatus must be placed so that the danger of collision is minimized. All apparatus should be firmly anchored in place. Permanent apparatus should be located in a separated area where it is less likely to create a hazard in the activity area. When not in use, all movable equipment and apparatus should be in a locked storage area, and access to this area should be controlled. The use of permanent apparatus should be permitted only under supervision.

The National Safety Council proposes the following procedures for the inspection of apparatus:

1. Apparatus in which wood is employed, such as slides, swings, teeters, and giant strides, should be inspected for worn or split portions or slivers.

2. All apparatus should be examined for broken parts, rough corners, projecting corners or clamps, and loose joints, bolts, and fastenings.

3. Chains, ropes, fastenings, and clamps should be examined regularly for signs of deterioration or looseness.

4. All minor repairs and adjustments should be made immediately.

5. All unsafe apparatus should be removed or roped off so that it cannot be used while it is in a dangerous condition.

6. All needed repairs or parts should be reported to the principal at once.

7. All movable parts and connections should be frequently inspected and well lubricated. It is good practice to replace yearly the parts of apparatus subjected to the most strenuous wear.

8. All exposed surfaces should be treated regularly with a preservative coating. Metal surfaces may be painted and wood surfaces treated with linseed oil and varnished.[13]

Locker Rooms

Locker, shower, and drying room floors should be constructed of nonslip material. Regulations prohibiting running and roughhousing should be posted and enforced in these areas. Drying areas should be used so that the locker room floors do not become slippery. Showers should be equipped with mixing valves to prevent scalding. Floors should be kept continuously free from soap and other slippery substances. In general, a coach or physical education teacher should regard the locker room area as another part of the teaching area and supervise it accordingly. If the class is coeducational, provision must be made for the supervision of the locker room of the opposite sex. This should be a procedure established through consultation with the school administration.

Equipment

There is one more component of safe premises. In addition to considerations about the facility or area and the apparatus used, a physical education teacher or coach must periodically examine the equipment that is used and establish guidelines for the use of equipment. In the badminton case cited earlier in this chapter, the use of an outdoor, rubber-tipped shuttlecock instead of an indoor shuttlecock was a factor in the decision of the court. Two considerations about equipment are needed. First, is the equipment used for the activity appropriate and the best available for the price? Second, do your students have adequate personal equipment for the activity? In general, adequate protective equipment should be furnished to, and worn by, all contestants in those sports or activities that require it. It should be regularly and thoroughly inspected, and it should meet any existing standards. Proper equipment for the activity should be provided, maintained, inspected, and either repaired or replaced at regular intervals. Personal equipment such as shoes, socks, and athletic supporters should be clean and appropriate to the activity, and a teacher or coach needs to observe that it is so. As a general rule, the best quality, most efficient, and most protective equipment should be purchased.

3.9 PREVENTIVE MAINTENANCE

The key concept to emphasize in the inspection of areas, facilities, and equipment is that of preventive maintenance. This requires not only that one be diligent in seeking out potentially dangerous conditions or equipment, but that one actively remedy any dangerous conditions. The action to remedy potentially dangerous conditions is essential to reduce lawsuits and to protect oneself in case of lawsuits.

NOTES

1. *Mokovich* v. *Independent School District No. 22, St. Louis County,* 177 Minn. 446, 225 N.W. 292 (1929).

2. *Stevens* v. *Central School Dist. No. 1 of the Town of Ramapo,* 270 N.Y.S.2d 23, aff'd 21 N.Y.2d 780, 288 N.Y.S.2d 475, 235 N.E.2d 448.

3. *Rodrigues* v. *Seattle School Dist. No. 1,* 66 Wash.2d. 51, 491 P.2d 326 (1965).

4. *Handy* v. *Hadley-Luzerne Free School District.* 277 N.Y. 685, 14 N.E.2d 390 (1938).

5. *Scala* v. *City of New York,* 102 N.Y. Supp.2d 790 (Sup. Ct. 1951).

6. *Styer* v. *Reading,* 360 Pa. 212, 61 A.2d 382 (1948).

7. Don D. Seaton, Herbert J. Stack, and Bernard Loft, *Administration and Supervision of Safety Education* (New York: Macmillan, 1969), p. 253.

8. Chuck Leve, *Inside Racquetball* (Chicago: Henry Regnery 1973), p. 20.

9. Betty Van der Smissen, *Legal Liability of Cities and Schools for Injurites in Recreation and Parks* (Cincinnati: W.H. Anderson, 1968). Also 1975 Supplement to the same.

10. "Sports Injury Litigation," Paper Delivered at the Practising Law Institute Seminar, St. Francis Hotel, San Francisco, Ca., September 13-15, 1979).

11. The Athletic Institute and AAHPER, *Planning Facilities for Athletics, Physical Education, and Recreation* (Chicago: The Athletic Institute and AAHPER, 1974).

12. Seaton et al., *Administration and Supervision of Safety Education,* p. 257.

13. Ibid., p. 255.

4

SUPERVISION OF PHYSICAL EDUCATION AND SPORT ACTIVITIES

4.1 SUPERVISION

The most important duty of a teacher or coach is to control the activity taught or coached. This implies immediate and direct supervision of the activity area and such ancillary areas as shower and locker rooms. It also implies that the conduct of the activity is well planned and under the supervision of qualified personnel.

Nearly all lawsuits in physical education and sport allege inadequate supervision—the failure to fulfill the duties of a supervisor. More specifically, these allegations are made in reference to inadequate inspection of the facility and of inadequate equipment, planning, student evaluation, warning, emergency procedures, first aid, and specific supervision.

For the purposes of this text, supervision is a broad term meaning the direction of a learning experience in physical education or sport. Supervision includes all those things that should be done while teaching or coaching, including such specific duties as:

1. inspecting the facility;
2. planning for an activity;
3. evaluating students for injuries or incapacities prior to instruction;
4. matching or equating students for competition
5. providing adequate and proper equipment
6. warning of any dangers inherent in the activity;
7. informing students of emergency procedures;
8. controlling closely the activity itself;
9. rendering first aid and providing access to medical treatment.

4.2 GENERAL SUPERVISION

There are two concepts of supervision in operation as one teaches or coaches. The first of these is general supervision—an awareness on the part of the supervisor of conditions which are or may become dangerous. Just as a school district is not an ensurer of safety, a teacher is not expected to supervise personally or closely every student every moment of every day. Teachers and coaches are expected to be diligent in providing ordinary care for their students' safety. Teachers and coaches are expected to behave as reasonable and prudent teachers and coaches would in providing a safe place. General supervision may refer to any part of the teacher's school day; specific supervision focuses more on instruction.

4.3 SPECIFIC SUPERVISION

Specific supervision refers to those actions one takes when planning, directing, and evaluating an activity. Specific supervision usually occurs during the instructional phase of an activity. If a teacher stops an act of rowdyism while walking down the hallway, the teacher has fulfilled a general supervisory duty. If a teacher inspects the support for a horizontal bar prior to its use, the teacher has performed a specific supervisory duty. Most teaching and coaching duties require specific supervision: the need to continuously ascertain that an activity is safely learned and performed.

Two cases illustrate the importance of both general and specific supervision. In *Stanley v. Board of Education,* the issue was the safety of a playground where the defendant was injured.[1] In this case, the plaintiff was playing in an elementary school yard in a summer recreational program. This program included both outdoor and indoor activities and was under the direction of a physical education teacher with some junior assistants. At the time of injury, the playground was under the supervision of one of the junior assistants, and the adequacy of this general supervision was questioned. Several activities were taking place simultaneously on the playground. Four boys started a game of fastpitch baseball and asked the plaintiff to move. He did, so that he was about twenty-five to thirty feet from the fastpitch game. The fastpitch players were using a bat that was not taped and that had a frayed knob at the bottom of the handle. The player was swinging very hard when the bat left his hands and ricocheted off a building, striking the plaintiff in the head. Two points of specific supervision examined were the closeness of the activities and the use of a possibly defective bat. The plaintiff won this case and was awarded $40,000.

In *Styer v. Reading* the court determined that the general conditions of play and the use of unsuitable equipment made playing badminton a dangerous activity.[2] In this case, discussed in Chapter 3, a playground leader failed to warn or stop two students from batting an outdoor, rubber-tipped badminton shuttlecock back and forth in a small, crowded, and poorly lighted room, without the use of a net. A duty of general supervision would have been to disallow the activity in the area, as the area was inappropriate. A lapse of a specific supervisory duty occurred when the activity was allowed without either a net or the proper shuttlecock. As a result of this injury, the plaintiff lost the sight of one eye and won an award from the court.

4.4 IMPACT OF FEDERAL LEGISLATION ON SUPERVISION

Ever since federal funds have been channeled into state and local educational programs, there has been a degree of federal influence over local educational programs. This is true today and certainly true of the supervisory duties of teachers and coaches. Three of the more important pieces of federal legislation affect supervision in regards to identifying abused children, educating handicapped children, and providing equal opportunity for both sexes in physical education, intramural, and extracurricular athletic programs.

The Child Abuse Prevention and Treatment Act

This 1974 federal legislation (42 U.S.C.S. Par. 5101 et seq—P.L. 93-247) asks teachers and coaches to identify abused children. This law recognizes child abuse as a major social problem and requires public officials to report any instance where there is reason to believe that a child has had serious injury or injuries inflicted upon him. Some states have amended this to allow the reporting of more subtle forms of child abuse. A Montana law, for instance, only provides that "reasonable cause to suspect" child abuse is necessary.[3] Included among those Montana professionals and officials required to report suspected child abuse are school teachers, other school officials, and employees who work during regular school hours. Any official in Montana who does not report possible child abuse is civilly liable for harm done to the child. The new law creates a duty to report. It also provides some protection, as the identity of professionals and officials making reports remains confidential. In addition, anyone investigating or reporting incidents, participating in judicial proceedings, or furnishing hospital or medical records as required is immune from any liability, civil or criminal, that might otherwise be imposed, unless that person acted in bad faith or with malicious purpose.

It is important for physical education teachers and coaches to understand their duties under this law, because it is quite likely they will be the first school officials to notice symptoms of child abuse, either in the locker room or on the court. Lethargic play and physical bruises are observable.

Assistance for Education of All Handicapped Act

This law (20 U.S.C.S. Par. 1411 et seq. —P.L. 94-142) is designed to assure that all handicapped children have a free, appropriate public education available to them. Included in this is the assurance that all handicapped children are educated to the maximum degree possible with their nonhandicapped peers in the least restrictive environments (mainstreaming). Interestingly, instruction in physical education is the only curricular area included in this law's description of special education. Further, this law asks that extracurricular services and activities be provided so that handicapped children have an equal opportunity for participation in such activities.

The implications of this law regarding supervision are obvious. Teachers are required to include children in the regular activities of the class whenever possible. Since the supervisory duties of physical education teachers and coaches include both the necessity to determine existing incapacities and injuries prior to activity and the necessity to insure that students are not overmatched or placed in inequitable competition with other students, more care and more planning are essential. One must become more judicious in selecting and modifying activities. One must be more aware of the limitations on performance created by a handicap. One must be even more diligent when supervising an activity so that it can be played safely by as many students as possible.

At this writing, it is impossible to determine the effect of this law on interscholastic athletics. Barred from playing athletics because of a handicap, several people have filed lawsuits against coaches, schools, and athletics associations. The results of these lawsuits have been mixed, but reasonable restrictions have been allowed, particularly if supported by the American Medical Association.

Title IX of the Educational Amendments Act of 1972

The purpose of this legislation is to prohibit sex discrimination in education, by far the most actively litigated aspect of rules governing extracurricular activities, especially in high school athletics.[4] Title IX (20 U.S.C.S., Par. 1681 et seq. — P.L. 92-318) provides that no person on the basis of sex shall be "excluded from participation in, be denied the benefits of or be treated differently from another person or otherwise be discriminated against" in educational programs, including interscholastic sports. While the interpretation and implementation of Title IX regulations are being challenged — and no final answers are as yet available — it appears safe to say that participants in physical education classes, intramurals, and interscholastic athletic programs must be evaluated for participation on the basis of ability. Initially, Title IX allowed separation by sex within those activities designated as contact sports, such as wrestling, boxing, rugby, ice hockey, football, and basketball. This separation is now under question, and teams must be selected on the basis of skill. This, in turn, may make the task of matching and equating students more difficult.

There are a number of lawsuits involving equal opportunities in athletics. Two of the more interesting cases occurred in Washington and Pennsylvania. In the first case, the question was whether a school district operating a high school in the State of Washington may constitutionally deny two of its fully qualified high school students permission to play on the high school football team in interscholastic competition solely on the ground the students are girls.[5] The students in this case had been allowed to try out for and practice with the boys' football team. The coach testified that both girls had in general been able to hold their own with the boys in practices, and would be allowed to play in games were it not for a Washington Interscholastic Activities Association regulation prohibiting girls from participating in interscholastic contact football on boys' teams. The Supreme Court of Washington found that such a rule was unconstitutional and that fully qualified high school students could not be denied the opportunity to play high school football solely on the ground that the students are girls.

In a similar case in Pennsylvania, the Commonwealth, through the state attorney general, initiated a lawsuit against the Pennsylvania Interscholastic Athletic Association because of one of its bylaws, which states "girls shall not compete or practice against boys in any athletic contest."[6] This bylaw was declared unconstitutional, and the P.I.A.A. was ordered to permit girls to practice and compete with boys in interscholastic athletics. The court added:

> Although the Commonwealth in its complaint seeks no relief from discrimination against female athletes who may wish to participate in football and wrestling, it is apparent that there can be no valid reason for excepting those two sports from our order in this case.

Not surprisingly, boys are now attempting to apply the same logic while trying out for girls' teams. The results thus far have been mixed. The summer 1980 issue of "Sports and the Courts" cited three cases as example.[7] In Rhode Island, the courts eventually ordered a high school to either create a volleyball team for boys or let a male student play on the girls' team. Since the boy had graduated by the time the decision was made, the point was moot, but interesting. In Massachusetts, the state board of education, through the attorney general, tested a Massachusetts Interscholastic Athletic Association amendment to a rule. This amendment provided:

With due regard to protecting the welfare and safety of all students participating in MIAA Athletics:

1. No boy may play on a girls' team.
2. A girl may play on a boys' team if that sport is not offered in the school for the girl.

The court did not foresee major problems if boys played on girls' teams, since there were few difficulties when girls joined boys' teams. It declared that the amended rule was invalid under the Massachusetts law. The court did not anticipate boys rushing headlong to participate on girls' teams. It encouraged a period of experimentation and imagination, along with tolerance, to solve the problems. The court also recommended a limit on the number of boys on girls' teams, or a quota for the number of boys who could participate in a given game.[8] Another state saw the issue differently than did Rhode Island and Massachusetts. In Illinois, a court concluded that the only sensible way to provide legitimate competition in volleyball for girls was to limit participation to girls only. It had no trouble finding that a separate girls' volleyball team served the government objective because it met the due process requirement by: "maintaining, fostering and promoting athletic opportunities for girls." Although there was an interesting dissent to this opinion, the gender-based classification was allowed.[9]

It appears that the only type of segregation allowed in physical education and sport is that based on the results of objective tests of ability. Despite the other turmoil surrounding the implementation of Title IX, this appears axiomatic. (See Appendix A, Summary of Significant Cases Involving Women in Sport.)

4.5 INSPECTION OF THE FACILITY

As discussed earlier, specific supervision refers to the planning, direction, and evaluation of a specific activity—that which is normally regarded as "instruction." One of the duties of specific supervision mentioned in Chapter 3 was the necessity of providing safe premises. This means that the facility, equipment, and apparatus used for the activity taught must be regularly and thoroughly inspected and made safe. The degree of inspection necessary is arbitrary, but if standards or recommendations from recognized experts in various activities are available, they should be utilized. The duty of inspecting a facility includes all areas that could be involved in the conduct of the activity. It is important to remember that an instructor has the responsibility for actual and constructive notice. Not only is an instructor responsible for dangerous conditions that are apparent, but also for those that *should have been noticed* by a reasonable and prudent professional. The concept of constructive notice is particularly worrisome, as any safety survey of an activity area will reveal a large number of items and conditions that could possibly be hazardous. One must try to provide a safe environment, but not cry "wolf" too often.

Gross disregard of this duty occurred in a Minnesota case in 1929.[10] In this case, the plaintiff was a high school football player at the defendant high school. He was injured at a football game conducted by the school district as a part of its educational program. The charge was that the defendant's officers and agents negligently used unslaked lime to mark the lines on the football field. During the game the plaintiff was thrown to the ground, and his face was forced into the lime, with the result that the sight of one eye was destroyed and that of the other eye seriously impaired. This case was not won by the plaintiff, due in large part to the strength of the defense of governmental immunity in effect in 1929. A similar case today would probably be won by the plaintiff. In some cases the theory of *res ipsa loquitur* would be applicable. This presumption, which literally means "the thing speaks for itself," allows recovery if both the cause of the accident was under the control of the defendant and the accident would not ordinarily have occurred without negligence on the part of the defendant. The theory is frequently applied when specific acts of negligence cannot be established by the plaintiff.

A second case illustrates the need for more subtle inspection of a facility. In this case, the plaintiff was a thirty-year-old playing basketball in a community recreation program.[11] The game was played in a building which was owned by the school district and which was a combination cafeteria, assembly, and gymnasium. Behind one of the baskets on the court was a door with a glass panel. While the plaintiff was running to make a shot, his momentum carried him beyond the end line into the door behind the basket. In trying to brace himself, the plaintiff put his arm through the pane of glass. He sued, and the court ruled that he was an invitee to whom the defendant owed a duty to use reasonable care for his protection and safety. A verdict was returned in plaintiff's favor for the sum of $15,000. The court concluded that the glass pane in the door should have been made of unbreakable glass (even though the architect did not believe so, the building had been used as a basketball court for fifteen years with no previous breakage of glass panes, and the plaintiff had voluntarily played in the court on at least seven prior occasions).

These two examples are not extreme. A teacher or coach needs to inspect carefully, regularly, and thoroughly the facilities used for instruction, and needs to learn to look for both the obvious and the subtle danger areas. Since so many of the areas used in physical education and sport programs are multiple-use areas, it is a good idea to conduct these inspections from a sport-specific state of mind and ask "What is there present in this facility that creates the potential for injury in this sport?" Practice the concept of *preventive maintenance*, and maintain facilities, apparatus, and equipment so that the risk of injury is minimized.

4.6 PLAN

Since planning should precede all that is done in physical education and sport instruction, it may appear trite to have a separate section on the topic. The point is that planning is sometimes ignored, and programs are sometimes "throw out the ball" activities. They should not be.

Books are written on planning in education. Anyone who has completed a program of teacher certification in physical education is familiar with curriculum plans, unit plans, and lesson plans. Most people who have completed a program of teacher certification in the 1970s have likely learned how to plan by using performance objectives. The purpose of this section is not to review the techniques regarding planning, but to reinforce the development of adequate written plans.

An adequate plan is one capable of withstanding professional scrutiny. Dougherty and Bonanno, in their excellent *Contemporary Approaches to the teaching of Physical Education*, make the following comments about planning.

The best written plans are only as good as a teacher's ability to implement them. Beautifully designed lessons, carefully typed to impress a principal or college supervisor are of no value if they cannot be implemented on the floor of the gymnasium. If the plans are not meaningful in terms of actual teaching, then they are an exercise in futility. Teachers should never put anything in their plans that they do not fully intend to carry out, and if subsequent evaluations show that certain aspects of the lesson are consistently omitted or bungled, one must ask why. Having once ascertained that a problem exists, the question becomes: Is the problem due to faulty planning or to some other factor? The following questions should assist the teacher in making that decision:

1. Are your goals realistic and attainable?
2. Have you considered:
   pupil background and ability levels?
   student interest?
   student attitudes toward the subject matter and you?
   your own interest and enthusiasm for the subject?
3. Do you know your subject matter well enough?
4. With regard to the subject matter:
   was it too easy or too easy or too difficult?
   did you make allowances for individual differences?
   was it made interesting and meaninful to the students?
   was there sufficient variety?
5. With regard to teaching style:
   were you comfortable with the teaching style?
   were your students ready to accept the realtive degree of
     freedom or limits imposed upon them?
   did you modify unsuccessful techniques during the lesson?
   did you utilize a variety of styles?
   did you make provisions for variations in learning rates?
6. With regard to organization and administration of the lesson:
   were your explanations and directions clear and concise?
   did your pupils understand exactly what was expected of
     them?
   were you well prepared?
   did you have emergency plans for rainy weather?
   did you know where the classes should be at all times and
     how they should get there?
   did they know this?
   were your classes ready to begin on time? If not, why?
   was all equipment ready and in good repair when needed?
   did you provide for the most efficient distribution of equip-
     ment and materials?
   how efficiently organized were such things as roll taking,
   locker room procedures, and post-class cleanup and return
   of equipment?
   have you analyzed each class in terms of discipline and your
     role in controlling it?

If the answers to any of these questions are unsatisfactory,
then one should begin the process of self-improvement by planning the necessary adjustments and then diligently practicing
their implementation.[12]

From *Contemporary Approaches to the Teaching of Physical Education,* 1979,
p. 120, by Dougherty and Bonanno, Burgess Publishing Company, Minneapolis, Minnesota. Reprinted by permission of the publisher.

Specific lawsuits alleging improper planning are numerous, except that planning (or lack of it) is behind all that occurs in physical education and sport instruction. In a case currently at trial, an allegation of improper planning has been made. This case involves the activity of pyramid-building in an elementary school. The teacher did plan for the activity, at least to the extent of using a textbook on elementary physical education activities to determine if the activity was appropriate. She used a reference, but the reference was forty-four years old. Depending on the activity, an old reference could make a crucial difference. Old textbooks may recommend activities no longer appropriate, such as those involving swinging rings, trampoline, and boxing. What was once appropriate may have since been modified, and it is an instructor's duty to know this and plan accordingly.

Six cases are cited in this section. Two indicate a gross lack of planning, and four focus on a more subtle point of planning. In the first case, the plaintiff and another young man were instructed by the defendant teacher to box three rounds of one minute each with a minute of rest between rounds.[13] The students had received no training in boxing but went at it "as hard as we could." The defendant teacher sat in the bleachers during the match. The plaintiff suffered a cerebral hemorrhage and subsequently underwent two operations. The lack of any training, particularly in a violent sport, and the lack of close supervision of the activity itself, clearly indicate inadequate planning on the part of the instructor.

The second case involved poor planning for an initiation ceremony into a lettermen's club.[14] At these annual initiations, the candidates for membership were given an electric shock which was produced by means of running electric wires connected with batteries through a transformer which reduced the current. In the 1941 initiation ceremony, the transformer was not available and electric current was obtained not from batteries but from an electric light socket. Each boy was brought separately into the gymnasium, asked to lie on an electrically wired mat, and then either handed a glass of water or had a glass placed upon his chest. The current was then turned on, the result being that the boy receiving the shock would respond and the glass of water would either spill over him or on the floor. In this ceremony, the fourth candidate to receive the electric shock complained that it was very strong. The next candidate was brought into the room, placed upon the wired mat, and the current was turned on. The student died immediately upon receiving this electric shock. The coach was held liable.

The previous two cases illustrate rather obvious errors in planning. A less noticeable error was charged in a 1965 Washington case where the plaintiff was injured while attempting to perform an exercise prescribed by the teacher.[15] The plaintiff claimed that the defendants were negligent in directing her to do the exercises, in failing to supervise properly, and in requiring her to perform acts which they knew or should have known she was incapable of performing safely without first giving her proper instructions. In other words, activities should be planned on the basis of the abilities of the students, and teachers and coaches should know what each and every student is capable of doing.

Fair enough, but the well-known *Bellman* case carries this planning dutya bit further.[16] In this case, the student wastrying to do a gymnastic stunt known as the "roll over two," in which the performer takes a short run, and dives over two persons who are on their hands and knees, alights on outstretched arms, and, with the head curled under in order to complete a forward roll, comes to a standing position. While trying to accomplish this feat, the plaintiff struck her head. The teacher testified that proper performance of the exercise depends not only upon a girl's agility and muscular strength, but also upon her mental attitude. The plaintiff indicated to the jury that she took the tumbling class work under protest; that the physical education teacher gave her no instruction directly but that she was shown how to do the exercises by advanced students in the class; that in doing the "roll over two" she had many times fallen on top of the girls on the floor; that she had a bad knee that "went out" at times; that two weeks before the accident she had fallen in the locker room and that the physical education teacher had dressed her knee with hot compresses; and that she had then told the teacher that her knee was bad and that she did not want to take tumbling. The court then stated that:

> This and other evidence, if believed by the jury is sufficient to support a verdict for the respondent either upon the theory that the "roll over two" is not an exercise suitable for senior high school girls, or that appellant's employees knew or should have known that because of the respondent's mental or physical condition she was not a proper subject for such instruction. . . .

In a vigorous dissent it was pointed out that on the day of the accident the student voluntarily went to her teacher, told her she had accomplished the stunt and was ready for her test, and asked the teacher to observe her for her marking. This dissent further stated:

> The opinion is unfair to the school district and to the entire structure of education throughout the state. No district and no teacher can tell whether physical education is condemned as

negligence in all cases, or whether it is the duty of the teacher to examine and know the physical and mental condition of every pupil, and assume liability if any injury occurs to a pupil by reason of such physical and mental condition at any time and at any place. . . . Courses in physical education will thus be curtailed or eliminated, depending on the degree of "guess" indulged by the school authorities on what a jury would say about it.

In the *Keesee* case, improper planning was alleged because the teacher deviated from a syllabus.[17] The class was playing a game of line soccer on a gymnasium floor area of about sixty by fifty feet. The school syllabus provided that the game be played by boys in two teams of about ten to twenty players each, in a space of about thirty by forty feet, and that each team consist of guards and one forward. The syllabus also indicated that the forwards, standing at the center line, were to try to gain possession of the ball and then advance it through the opposing guards by dribbling and kicking it. Instead the teacher divided the class of girls into two teams of twenty to twenty-two students each, and assigned them numbers so that when one number was called four students from each team would race out toward the center line and attempt to gain possession of the ball. The teacher's testimony that the necessary skill to play the game could be developed in one session was rejected by the court as "incredible." The court stated that:

the evidence requires a conclusion that, by direction of the teacher, from six to eight novices, including plaintiff, converged on the ball, at a run, in two numerically equal—or nearly equal—groups and, on meeting, kicked away, inexpertly and without either self-imposed or externally visited restraint, in a lively effort to gain its possession and that during the action plantiff was kicked by another player and was injured as a direct or indirect result of the kick. That an injury would result to someone from the melee ensuing of such occasions was, if not inevitable, at least reasonably foreseeable.

Whenever a planned course of study, such as a syllabus, is changed and less restrictive rules (sometimes called "jungle rules") are used, these changes must be planned so that a dangerous activity is avoided. Students must have adequate preparation for any rule changes.

A 1979 Nebraska case illustrates the importance of proper planning. This case is interesting because it involves a student teacher and tragic in that it involves the death of a student in a golf class.[18] A fourteen-year-old ninth grader was struck unconscious by a golf club swung by a fellow student and died two days later. In this school, mandatory golf instruction during physical education classes began on a Monday. The decedent was absent from school that day, and his first exposure to the program was when his class next met on Wednesday, the day of the accident. Classes on both dates were conducted in the school gymnasium because of inclement weather. Instruction was coeducational, and one male teacher and one female teacher were responsible for providing supervision and instruction. On the day of the accident the male teacher was not present. His place was take by a student teacher who had been at the school for approximately five weeks and who had assisted with four to six golf classes on the previous two days. In the gymnasium twelve mats were placed across the width of the gym, in two rows of six each. One row of mats was located in the south half of the gym and the other row in the north half. The mats measured about two feet square and were spaced ten to twelve feet apart. A golf club and three or four plastic "wiffle" balls were placed by each mat.

The students were divided into groups of four or five students and each group was assigned to use of one of the mats. The boys hit the golf balls in a southerly direction and the girls in a northerly direction. At the start of the class all the students were to sit along the center line of the basketball court between the two rows of mats. On the signal of one of the instructors one student from each group would go up to the assigned mat, tee up a ball, and wait for the signal to begin. After the student had hit all of the balls on the mat he was to lay the club down and return to the center of the gym. When all of the students were back at the center line, the next student in each group was directed to retrieve the balls and the procedure was repeated.

The students had been told to remain behind a certain line on the gym floor when they were not up at the mats. The female teacher was working with the girls in the class while the male student teacher was working with one of the male students. The decedent, who prior to the date of his death had never held a golf club in his hands, had difficulty and asked another student to help him. Another student came forward, showed the decedent how to grip the club and told him that he would take two practice swings and then hit the ball. The decedent moved away and stood about ten feet behind the other student. The demonstrating student looked over his shoulder to observe the decedent before taking two practice swings and then stepped up to the ball and took a full swing at it. Unaware that the decedent had moved closer, he hit the decedent with the club on the follow through.

In the discussion of the case a great deal of attention was given to the manner in which the class was planned. The student teacher acknowledged that it was not until after the accident that he realized the class arrangement was different from what was recommended. The student teacher also testified that he had received no instruction from any of the regular teachers or faculty prior to the commencement of the class, nor did he have a lesson plan, nor did he give any oral instruction to any of the students as a whole.

The plaintiff called for testimony from a retired gym teacher with a B.A. degree in Physical Education. This former instructor said that he would have used a different procedure for teaching golf. He testified that the teacher should be supervising and keeping an eye on all students using the mats; that if the teacher noticed a student having difficulty or needing specialized instruction, the teacher should blow the whistle, call the class to a halt, and stop the students from talking so as to gain their control and attention. Then the teacher should demonstrate to the one student in need while all the other students watched and listened, and thereby, in effect give a public lesson to all in attendance. The award of $50,000.00 to the estate of the deceased student was affirmed by the Supreme Court of Nebraska.

4.7 EVALUATE STUDENTS FOR INJURY OR INCAPACITY

It is important that students not be placed into inappropriate activities. As earlier indicated by the *Bellman* case, this evaluation should include the physical and mental state of the student. Just as an injured student should not be expected to perform an activity potentially harmful to one with that injury, neither should a student with valid apprehensions about an activity be forced to perform that activity.

All evaluations should be based on a medical examination of the student by a physician. Since these are usually yearly screening physicals, teachers and coaches need to exercise an additional degree of care in observing injuries or incapacitating circumstances that demand a temporary adjustment in one's exercise program. It is sometimes necessary to develop individualized educational programs for those students with more serious or persistent injuries. At present, a goal for teachers and coaches is the "mainstreaming" of as many students as possible. This mainstreaming must be done safely. It may require the modification of activities so that more students may enjoy the benefits of exercise, and whenever activities are modified, rules for safe play may need to be modified. Whenever the range of abilities is increased, as it may be by the mainstreaming of students, the possibility of mismatch or inequitable competition is increased. This, in turn, demands more diligent planning and observation by the teacher or coach.

One additional point needs to be emphasized. Injuries heal, incapaciting conditions improve, and these injuries and conditions affect play more in some activities than in others. In other words, a dynamic situation exists and teachers and coaches must be flexible enough to avoid a common error. This is the error of regarding a student with a condition that incapacitates him in one activity as being incapacitated in all activities. The potential for stereotyping exists. This can be avoided only by a continuous professional assessment of the degree of incapacitation an injury causes for that activity at that time. Continuous observation, regular evaluation, and flexible planning are required.

An Oregon case in 1971 illustrates the problem. In this case, the school district required all students, unless excused by a doctor, to earn a certain number of physical education credits as a requisite to high school graduation.[19] The plaintiff was excused from all physical education for the last half of her freshman year because of a back problem. During her sophomore year, she was excused by her doctor from doing sit-ups. The student then was injured while jumping from an elevated board which rested on a coiled spring, touching her toes in the air, and landing on her feet. Plaintiff lost her balance and fell backward, suffering a compression fracture of two vertebrae. The exercise was required. The doctor had earlier requested a list of the exercises and gymnastics the plaintiff was required to perform at school. Although this request was made at least four different times, the last being about one week prior to the accident, the list was never provided. The court held that the school was bound by information it would have had, if it had exercised due diligence and provided the list of exercises. The doctor would have recommended against plaintiff performing this exercise. According to the court:

> A person is bound not only by what he knows but also by what he might have known had he exercised ordinary diligence.

This illustrates the concept of constructive notice.

A 1934 California case provides an interesting commentary on the duty of determining incapacities and on the duty of supervising "free play" activities.[20] In this case, the student was engaged in a game of basketball during a period of "free play." This free-play basketball was supervised generally by the instructor without adhering to the strict rules of a regular game. It was also the intructor's duty to supervise other similar activities conducted at the same time. The student had been instructed with regard to the rules of free-play basketball and fully understood the game. He was sixteen, weighed 140 pounds, and was described as a "vigorous, robust boy." He was a very ambitious and active student and was considered a proficient basketball player. During the game, the student was struck on the forehead by the basketball. He was seen to stoop over and rub his forehead. He then left the game and sat upon a bench. The instructor did not know that the student had been injured. The student was later found unconscious in the dressing room. He was taken to the hospital, where he died the following day. An autopsy revealed a preexisting aneurism of a cerebral artery. A suit for damages was tried and resulted in a verdict in favor of the plaintiff, the student's father, for the sum of $15,700. The court rendered a contrary verdict which was upheld on appeal, in part because no one knew or could have been expected to know that the student possesed an aneurism. The court stated:

> The presence and supervision of a referee in basket ball (sic) games do not prevent irregular plays. The referee merely regulates the game and penalizes foul plays. There are certain hazards and unavoidable accidents which occur in all such athletic sports against which a referee may not guard by the greatest degree of caution. Even if the whistle had been blown when the ball went out of bounds at the time this occurred, it is not unlikely that it would have been returned in the same manner and that the student would have been struck in the forehead by the ball just as he was struck in that unfortunate play. We are unable to say this accident would not have occurred under the enforcement of the strict rules of a regular game, and those rules were not invoked in a "free play" game. Ordinary prudence would not necessarily require such rules for the safety of the students. There is no evidence that the instructor omitted to perform any duty at the time of this accident which became the proximate cause thereof. It was a deplorable tragedy and the grievous results thereof invoke the sympathy of all. It was, however, not attributable to the negligence of the instructor and liability of the school district therefore does not follow:

In summary, there is no firm guideline, no consistent legal trend that enables a teacher or coach to know which injuries or incapacitating conditions he is responsible for observing. The students must be in proper physical condition, prepared, and in a proper state of mind for the activity.

4.8 MATCH OR EQUATE STUDENTS IN COMPETITION

Several lawsuits have alleged that students have been mismatched while playing a sport. These suits have not been limited to contact sports but have occurred in some activities deemed noncontact. It appears that more care must be taken in pairing or matching students in most activities because contact, inherent or not, may occur.

As a result, many of the traditional methods of quickly and easily dividing students into teams should be used with discretion. The convenience of having the seventh grade play the eighth grade, of dividing the students by alternating numbers, of dividng the students on the basis of height, indeed any arbitrary method of placing students into teams to lay a sport is questionable. Compounding the difficulty of this task is the presence of inconsistent court decisions. A technique of choosing competitors held to be reasonable and prudent in one jurisdection has not been so held in another.

It seems safe to say that any separation of students into teams should not be based on just one factor, particularly if that factor is convenience. A number of factors should be considered. Perhaps first one should consider the skill and experience of the students in the activity. While pairing students on this basis is good, the principle of specificity should be remembered. A student good in one activity is not necessarily good in all activities. Matching by such personal factors as age, maturity, weight, and height must be considered. As demonstrated in the *Bellman* case, the mental condition of the student must not be ignored, nor should the presence of any injuries that may temporarily hinder a student's ability to perform. There are many other factors to be considered, many of them sport-specific, and it is the task of the teacher or coach to consider judiciously all that is relevant in matching students.

Even the voluntary activity of competitive sports is not spared. In an Oregon case, the court stated that:

> It is possible that two football teams may be so disparate in size and ability that those responsible for supervising the athletic program would violate their duty in permitting the teams to play.[21]

In this case the plaintiff had been sent into a football game with another school from the same county. The plaintiff was an inexperienced football player, a freshman who weighed approximately 140 pounds and "wasn't very coordinated." The complaint alleged that the other team consisted of very large boys and a highly experienced rough team, all of which the defendant school district knew, or should have known. The court in this case rejected the contention of unequal competition and stated:

> Most boys who play high school football begin as plaintiff did, by going out for the team as a freshman. Most of them are "uncoordinated" as plaintiff was alleged to have been at the time he played. To say that it is improper for the officials of the school to permit such "inexperienced" and "uncoordinated" boys to play would be the equivalent of saying that football could not properly be a part of the athletic program of any high school in the state because the program could never lawfully be started.

Another case alleging improper matching of students occurred in New York. In this case, the plaintiff, a seventh grader, was kicked by another boy during the play of a game described as soccer, as a result of which he was knocked to the floor and struck the back of his head.[22] The game was being played in the gymnasium under the supervision of the physical education teacher. The teacher had placed a group of twenty boys on one side of the gymnasium, another group of twenty on the other side, and then a ball in the middle of the gymnasium floor. Each boy in one group was given a number and his counterpart in the other group was given a similar number. When the instructor would call a particular number the two boys to whom that number was assigned would run toward each other as rapidly as they could for the purpose of kicking the ball toward the desired goal. The boys were about seventy-five feet apart when they began to run toward each other. The teacher testified that the boys participating in the game all came from the same grade, admitted that he picked them out at random and made no effort to match up boys of the same general height or weight. According to the court:

> The infant plaintiff testified that his opposite number was about 6 feet tall and weighed about 180 or 190 pounds, thus making it apparent, from seeing the infant plaintiff five years later at the trail, that he was practically a baby compared to his erstwhile opponent at the time of the accident.

The plaintiff was awarded damages.

On the other hand, in a California case a convenient method of choosing sides was upheld. The injury occurred in a game of touch football during the noon recess period.[23] As was customary in free-play games, the participants were not selected according to age, size, or weight. As a consequence, the players ranged in weight from 85 to 190 pounds. At the time of the accident, the student was a member of the eighth grade team. Teams were selected on the basis of grade, and in this game the eighth grade was playing the seventh grade. One boy from each team was captain and chose the team members. A student, 5'4" and 97 pounds, blocked another student 5'10" and 145 pounds. The plaintiff was struck in the abdomen by the other student's knee and later had his spleen and one kidney removed. The Supreme Court of California, in reversing an earlier verdict, held that the selection of players for free-play games according to grades was a convenient and practical method of segregation:

> All the evidence is to the effect that touch football is not a dangerous or rough game. Several witnesses testified that, although the practice of matching the seventh against the eighth grade had been followed extensively throughout the county, they knew of no serious injury prior to the one to Pirkle. From this evidence, it must be concluded that the method of segregation employed by the defendants was a reasonable one.

In summary, it seems that methods of matching students based only on techniques of convenience are inadequate, and that a great deal more care is expected of teachers and coaches to match students on the basis of skill, height, weight, size, age, and experience. This duty is more difficult at present because of mandated coeducational physical education and sport programs and of mandated mainstreaming.

4.9 PROVIDE ADEQUATE AND PROPER EQUIPMENT

A sixteen-year-old football player broke his neck when he attempted to tackle an opponent.[24] As a result of the injury, the player is a permanent quadriplegic. He sued the company that manufactured the helmets for producing a defective product. A trial court agreed with him and awarded the player $5.3 million dollars and his father over $73,000 for medical expenses. Indeed, there has been a marked increase in football helmet cases in the past two decades, ironically because manufacturers of athletic equipment have developed more protective helmets and face masks. While these helmets are better at protecting the player against facial injury and concussion, they seem to cause a higher incidence of neck flexion and extension injuries. This increase in lawsuits involving equipment is not limited to contact sports. In Florida, there is an average of three lawsuits a week involving three-wheeled golf carts which easily tip over.[25] In some cases, a name used for a product has been changed because the name implied protection. Examples of these are the "safety" binding and "safety" strap in skiing. Unsupervised backyard trampolines and diving boards on homeowner's small pools are, in the words of an attorney active in such lawsuits, "almost indefensible."[26] The style of the activity may even be changed as illustrated by the nonsomersaulting techniques now advocated for trampolines.

It is apparent that the teacher or coach must become more diligent in the manner in which he or she selects, disperses, uses, and repairs equipment. Even such an apparently harmless item as a badminton shuttlecock has partially caused a successful lawsuit. In a 1971 Tennessee case, at issue was the absence of a piece of equipment that should have been present.[27] In this case, the plaintiff, an eighth-grade girl, was participating in a softball game along with other members of her class as part of the physical education program. The plaintiff was catching, and after another student hit the ball and started to run toward first base, the batter released the bat in such a manner that it flew back and struck the plaintiff in the face. Plaintiff required emergency room care. The school did furnish catcher's masks, but the students were not required to wear them. The case was decided for the plaintiff, appealed, and reversed by the Supreme Court of Tennessee. In discussing the equipment in question, the court said:

> As to the matter of requiring the catcher in a softball game to wear a mask, again we think it is common knowledge that the very nature of the game in question calls for the use of a soft ball as opposed to the regulation hard baseball and we also know that this game, which is played by many thousands of youngsters throughout the country, contemplates the pitching of a slow ball rather than the fast curve ball such as is thrown by baseball pitchers in the regular game of baseball.
>
> The evidence in the record before us indicates that plaintiff had played softball at home and at school many times, was a skilled player, and knew what she was doing. She testified that she had seen other batters sling the bat after striking the ball. There can be no question but that she was familiar with the risk she was taking when she got behind the bat to catch the ball. . . . Thus we find no satisfactory evidence of actionable negligence on the part of the school or its representatives in the failure to require the wearing of a mask by the plaintiff . . . .

If equipment is used it must be used properly. Some equipment has guidelines for its use. If these are available, they should be used. For example, the National Operating Committee for Standards in Athletic Equipment (NOCSAE) has published recommendations for football helmets. These are listed in Figure 4-1, and the National

Collegiate Athletic Association recommends that the list be displayed prominently in the football locker room and one copy of it be placed in each player's locker.

Fig. 4-1.

Football Helmet Inspection List

1. Check helmet fit for agreement with manufacturer's instructions and procedures.
2. Examine shell for cracks and replace any that have cracked. Do not use a helmet with a cracked shell.
3. Examine all mounting rivets, screws, Velcro and snaps for breakage, distortion and/or looseness. Repair as necessary.
4. Replace face guards that have become misshapen, causing shell distortion and resulting in a poor fit.
5. Examine for helmet completeness, and replace any parts which have become damaged, such as sweatbands, nose snubbers and chinstraps.
6. Replace jaw pads when damaged. Check for proper installation and fit.
7. Examine chinstrap for proper adjustment, and inspect to see if it is broken or stretched out of shape; also inspect the hardware to see if it needs replacement.
8. Read instructions provided by manufacturer regarding care and maintenance procedures. Always follow these instructions.
   CAUTION: Only paints, waxes, decals or cleaning agents approved by the manufacturer are to be used on any helmet. It is possible to get a severe or delayed reaction by using unauthorized materials, which could permanently damage the helmet shell and affect its safety performance.

Players

Inspect your particular style of helmet prior to each usage. Never wear a damaged helmet.

Suspension Style

Check hardware, i.e., screws or rivets that may be loose or missing.

Check webbing for tears in threads, stretching, or pulling away at rivet locations.

If crown webbing is adjustable, check that crown rope is properly adjusted and is tied tightly using a square knot.
Check interior padding for proper placement and good conditions.

Padded Style

Foam/Air/Liquid

Check foam padding for proper placement and signs of deterioration.
Check for cracks in vinyl/rubber covering of air, foam, liquid padded helmets.
Verify that protective system or foam padding has not been altered or removed.
Check all rivets, screws, Velcro and snaps to be sure they are properly fastened and holding protective parts.
If any of the above inspections indicate a need for repair or replacement, notify the proper authority. This is your reponsibility.
If recommendations for other equipment become available, they should be similarly posted.

The following guidelines are suggested for physical education teachers and coaches in regard to equipment.

1. Rationally select the best equipment your budget will allow, and buy only from reputable dealers.

2. Take great care in adjusting, fitting, and repairing all equipment, and make inaccessible all equipment not suitable for use, or not at present in use.

3. Present the necessary warnings to your students, to the point that they know, understand, and appreciate the potential risks of a game or a piece of equipment.

4. Rely upon reputable reconditioners to see that equipment is properly repaired or replaced.

5. Regularly and thoroughly inspect equipment.

6. Participate in and stay up to date with reports of injury-reporting systems and the equipment involved in injuries.

7. Be current as to changes in equipment and changes in technique in the activities you teach or coach. Teach the proper technique properly.

4.10 WARN OF DANGERS INHERENT IN THE ACTIVITY

Students should never be exposed to dangers that are not part of an activity. They should be warned of the dangers present in an activity, of the inherent risk that any game or sport has. The standard of care for a teacher or coach to offer is now to have the players know, understand, and appreciate the risks in an activity.[28] It is no longer sufficient to simply warn of risks; one must ensure that the risks are understood. It is unclear exactly what degree of understanding and appreciation participants must have, but it is safe to say that a one-time verbal warning may not be adequate.

An interesting example of the importance of warnings was presented at a conference on Sports Injury Litigation in 1979[29] In this case an experienced high school baseball player was severely injured while attempting to score on a squeeze play. The batter took a full swing and missed the ball entirely. The catcher caught the pitch and moved out to block home plate. The base runner charged intentionally into the catcher head first and injured himself. In the lawsuit, the injured student claimed that the school board failed to provide adequate and competent coaching, that the coach "carelessly and negligently trained, supervised, managed and controlled" the injured student, and the coach failed to properly teach and train the rudiments and fundamentals of the game. The injured student claimed that the risk of injury was enhanced or concealed by the omission to give explicit warnings to the players against charging into other players head first. In this case, evidence was presented, even by the injurd student, that the coach did affirmatively teach the correct technique (feet-first sliding), but did not warn against "radical and incompatible deviations from what was affirmatively and soundly taught." Further, in a similar play two weeks before the injury, the injured player had used his shoulder to bowl over a catcher and score the run—after which the coach allegedly praised him for his play. Despite the injured player's experience, his never having been taught the head-first slide, and his having been taught only the feet-first slide, the jury awarded $1,800,000 to the injured student, and $90,000 to his father.

Warnings should be given, and they should be repeated; hazardous conditions, safety rules, and other warnings should be written and posted whenever the situation warrants such action. If these warnings are written and posted, they should be continuously visible. As an ironic bad example, a recent visit to a swimming pool found warnings and safety rules present, but hidden from view by lifesaving equipment. The NOCSAE statement on football helmets, for example, should be posted inside the player's locker so that he will be constantly reminded of his responsibility in checking equipment to ensure that the helmet protects as it should to reduce the inherent danger of head and facial injuries in football.

An interesting case involving warnings occurred in New York. The Village of Lake Placid owned and maintained a public recreation area on the westerly shore of Mirror Lake, consisting of a wooded park, a sand beach, and a swimming dock.[30] The park area was lighted at night and open to the public continuously. The beach was open generally during daylight hours from June to September, and the Village employed lifeguards to supervise the use of the beach area. When the beach area was closed for swimming, the public was allowed to walk through the park and beach area and fish from the dock. There were four entrances to the beach but only one sign was used to close the beach, and that was usually placed on the right side of the beach house facing the water. The dock extended into an area of three to five feet of water depth, with no signs warning of water depth. About 2:00 a.m. the injured party sustained grievous injuries when he dived off the dock in shallow water and struck his head. He suffered a fracture of the fifth cervical vertebra, causing a compression of the spinal cord and rendering him a quadriplegic. The injured party admitted that he knew the dock was closed and that he was not supposed to be there. In supporting the lower court's verdict for the diver, the Appellate Division of the Supreme Court of New York said:

> The park area, beach and swimming dock admittedly had no barriers, real or suggested to dissuade visitors from venturing onto the dock when the beach was closed for swimming. . . .The presence of a single sign near the beach house where towels were rented was not a sufficient deterrent.

Three factors relevant to warnings were absent. First, there was an inadequate number of warnings of beach closure. Second, the one warning posted was not posted in a visible place. Third, the fishing dock should have had depth warnings on it.

Warnings must not be ambiguous. At a Practising Law Institute session on sport injury litigation, one attorney mentioned an accident involving a child from a country using the metric system who was injured because he thought three indicating a three-foot depth at a hotel pool meant three meters and would be safe for diving. The child knew of the warning, but he didn't understand it and couldn't therefore appreciate the potential danger of the area.

4.11 INFORM STUDENTS OF EMERGENCY PROCEDURES

Every teacher and coach must take the necessary steps to inform student-athletes of the procedures to follow in the event of an emergency. These procedures, regulations, and safety rules should be established for the entire school by the school administration. They should then be posted, discussed, and practiced so that prompt and correct response to an emergency may occur.

Two cases illustrate the point. In New Jersey, a teacher left the room to treat an injured student.[31] During his absence another student was injured. Before the teacher left the room he had warned the class not to use a springboard during his absence. While the teacher was gone, one of the students jumped off the springboard, landed incorrectly, and severely injured himself. He became permanently paralyzed. The plaintiff alleged that the injury was foreseeable, the springboard was a dangerous piece of equipment, that mats should have been placed near the springboard, along with a gymnastic belt to assist the students with springboard stunts, and that students should not have the responsibility to spot such an activity. The court ruled in favor of the plaintiff, and initially awarded him over one million dollars, a highly significant award in the early 1960s.

An interesting case occurred in Louisiana in 1970 in which it appeared that the coach simply ignored correct emergency procedures.[32] In this case, following a practice workout, a high school football player sustained heat stroke and exhaustion resulting in death. A district court dismissed plaintiffs' lawsuit and they appealed. The Court of Appeals held that high school football coaches who actively denied the student player access to treatment for some two hours after symptoms of heat stroke and shock appeared were guilty of negligence. The injury occurred in August during the second day of football practice. At approximately 5:20 p.m., while participating in wind sprints, the student became ill. He was assisted to the school bus, and there became nauseated. The bus arrived at the school twenty minutes later, and the student was helped into the school where he was placed on the cafeteria floor on a blanket. He appread pale, tired, and exhausted. The student was later given a shower and placed between two blankets. By this time (approximately 5:50) he was clammy, pale, and breathing heavily. The coaches brought a first aid book into the cafeteria and discussed what was wrong and what should be done with the student. At approximately 6:40 parents of another player arrived at the school and observed the injured student. They described him as appearing grayish-blue, with his mouth hanging slightly ajar, and as moaning. One parent stated to the coach that the student was critical, apparently in shock, and that a physician should be called. When the parent offered to call a physician, the coach told him not to, that he, the coach, would take care of it. The physician arrived at 7:15 and diagnosed the student's condition as profound heat exhaustion with shock to an advanced degree, but not necessarily irreversible. The student's condition continued to worsen, and he died around 2:30 the following morning. Testimony pointed out that the first aid rendered was not only delayed but improper, and the testifying physician stated the student's death would have been much more unlikely had he received proper medical treatment when he first informed the coach of his illness. The parents of the student were awarded damages of over $40,000.

4.12 SUPERVISE THE SPECIFIC ACTIVITY

The lack of supervision or inadequate supervision may not create liability, but the determining factor is whether or not such lack or inadequacy of supervision was the proximate cause of the injury.[33] There are a number of concerns regarding supervision expressed in lawsuits, including the nature of the supervision, the location of the supervisors, and the competency and adequacy in numbers of the supervisors. In playground or free-play activities, it is usually held that general rather than specific supervision is adequate. Specific supervision is normally required either for the first time instruction is being given for an activity or for an especially dangerous activity.[34] Since there are risks inherent in most if not all physical education and sport activities, it is expected that teachers and coaches closely supervise these activities, but it is not expected that teachers and coaches personally observe everything and guarantee the safety of the students. It is necessary that an activity be watched so that it does not become dangerous because of rowdyism, defective apparatus, unsafe areas, lack of protective equipment, and inappropriate activities for the maturity and skill of the students.

It is necessary to plan properly for supervision. In one case, the noon lunch period was supervised by three administrators and two teachers.[35] The areas around the gymnasium were the responsibility of the physical education teachers. Two boys began to slap box with each other just outside the gymnasium. After a few minutes, one boy fell backwards, hitting his head on the asphalt paving and fracturing his skull. He died a few hours later. The physical educator on duty had been in the gym office eating lunch. His desk faced away from the office windows, and a wall obscured his view of the area where the slap boxing occurred. The court said that the plan for supervision was defective because it lacked a comprehensive schedule of supervising assignments and instructions about expectations of supervising teachers.

Most of the concern about supervision occurs over the presence of teachers and coaches during an activity. It is not a requirement that a teacher be present, but it surely is a strong recommendation. There are instances where the absence of a teacher is justified. In one of these, a student was struck in the eye by a tennis ball while he and other members of the tennis team were playing handball in the gymnasium.[36] The coach had to prepare some tournament bracketings and had asked the boys to wait in the dressing room. Most of the boys began batting a tennis ball against the wall with their hands. Two of them went to the other side of the gym and used a tennis racket to swing at the ball as in baseball. One of these batted balls struck a student and caused serious injury to his eye. The court held that playing handball with a tennis ball was not an activity of inherent danger, and that the coach was performing work in the line of his duty and hence not negligent. This case must not be considered typical. More typical is the boxing case cited earlier in which two untrained students were allowed to engage in a vigorous boxing match while the teacher sat in the bleachers and did not intervene at any time, even after a student was staggered. This absence of supervision established negligence.

Negligence was also found when a fourteen-year-old student was injured by an act of rowdyism committed when the teacher was not present.[37] In this case, the student and forty-eight other boys reported to their physical education class. After checking attendance, the teacher told the boys to "shoot around" with basketballs. The teacher left the class unsupervised. After about ten minutes the game of basketball deteriorated into a game of "keep-away." The game ranged over at least half of the gym floor. The keep away game became rougher, involving pushing and tripping. The plaintiff was eventually injured when he was pushed into another student and fell to the floor. The Wisconsin Supreme Court reversed an earlier decision and found negligence, in part because:

> It does not seem inherently unreasonable to expect that teachers will be present in classes which they are entrusted to teach. This should not, of course, mean that a teacher who absents himself from a room is negligent as a matter of law. . . . What this means must depend upon the circumstances under which the teacher absented himself from the room. Perhaps relevant consi-

deration would be the activity in which the students are engaged, the instrumentalities with which they are working (band saw, dangerous chemicals), the age and composition of the class, the teacher's past experience with the class and its propensities, and the reason for and duration of the teacher's absence. Even if the teacher is found to be negligent, when the injury is the result of rowdyism or intentional conduct, the question of intervening and superseding cause arises, as does apportionment of negligence. The question will be whether, under all the circumstances, the teacher acted reasonably

A wrestling case in California contains a different allegation of inadequate supervision. In this case, a seventeen-year-old student in a wrestling class suffered a broken leg.[38] He alleged that the physical education instructor was negligent in directing the student, without giving him proper instruction, to wrestle with another student and in failing to supervise the wrestling. It was further alleged that the moving of the injured student to a sitting position in an automobile to remove him for medical attention resulted in a severed nerve which permanently crippled his foot. The case was resolved in favor of the defendant because the claim had not been filed against the defendant within the statutory time.

In a football case at Colgate University, the failure to teach correct technique was at issue.[39] While tackling a teammate in a football scrimmage, a freshman at Colgate suffered a broken neck and became a permanent quadriplegic. He sued, unsuccessfully, the Colgate coaching staff because they had taught him to tackle with his head.

In some cases, agents other than a teacher or coach are alleged to have inadequately supervised the activity. Such was the case in Washington involving a wrestling match.[40] In this case, the trial court was instructed that the referee was the agent of the school district, and that his standard of care was that of the ordinarily prudent referee. Near the end of the third round of a wrestling match between two boys, the injured student's opponent was attempting to pin him. In the course of this attempt, he was alternating half nelsons, first to one side and then to the other, trying to roll the plaintiff into a pin position. This process had taken the students to a corner of the main mat near where small side mats were placed against the main mat. The referee noticed a separation between the main mat and the side mat, and moved to close the gap to protect the contestants should they roll in that direction off the main mat onto the bare floor. In so doing, his attention was diverted from the participants for a moment. While his attention was so diverted, the plaintiff's opponent applied what appeared to be a full nelson for anywhere from one to ten seconds. Almost simultaneously the buzzer sounded the end of the round, the referee blew his whistle, and the opponent broke the hold after a final lunge. The plaintiff slumped to the mat, unable to move due to the severance of a major portion of his spinal cord resulting in permanent paralysis of all voluntary functions below his neck. The Supreme Court of Washington agreed with the trial court in instructingthe jury that if the referee was negligent, the school district must, as a matter of law, respond in damages. The earlier verdict in favor of the school district was reversed and sent back for retrial.

The task of supervising closely an activity encompasses numerous duties related to the proper instruction of an activity. Even if all of these instructional supervisory duties are discharged to the proper standard of care, injuries can occur, and lawsuits result. The object of closely supervising an activity is to eliminate dangers not inherent in the activity and reduce the risk intensity of dangers inherent in the activity. Sometimes, in spite of all that a teacher, coach, or official does, negligent acts occur. This is well illustrated by a recent case in which a soccer player sued an opponent for negligence.[41] This case involved a soccer match between two amateur teams of high school age. Approximately twenty minutes after play had begun, a player kicked the ball over the midfield line. Two players chased the free ball. One player passed the ball to the plaintiff, the goalie. The goalie went down on his left knee, received the pass, and pulled the ball to his chest. The defendant continued to run in the direction of the plaintiff and kicked the left side of the plaintiff's head. The court stated:

> When athletes are engaged in an athletic competition; all teams involved are trained and coached by knowledgeable personnel; a recognized set of rules governs the conduct of the competition; and a safety rule is contained therein which is primarily designed to protect players from serious injury, a player is then charged with a legal duty to every other player on the field to refrain from conduct proscribed by a safety rule.

It was the opinion of the court that a player is liable for injury in a tort action if his conduct is such that it is either deliberate, willful, or with a reckless disregard for the safety of the other player so as to cause injury to that player. The court ruled that the trial court erred in directing a verdict in favor of the defendant, and reversed and remanded the case for a new trial. This case is decidedly different from other player v. player cases which are usually assaults. This case involves a tort action for negligence.

4.13 RENDER FIRST AID AND PROVIDE ACCESS
TO MEDICAL TREATMENT

The *Mogabgab* case cited earlier, in which a football player died of heat exhaustion, is a good example of failure to carry out the duty of rending adequate first aid. All teachers, coaches, athletic trainers, and recreation leaders should take first aid courses and have periodic first aid refreshers. In addition, every school and every program that includes physical education or sport activities should have a plan for obtaining the necessary medical care for injuries. This program should be developed through the cooperation of the school board, the school administration, and the faculty. Further, once this program is developed, it should be disseminated and practiced. It is an error to allow such a program to hide in a seldom used teacher's handbook. It is the responsibility of all school officials to be aware of this program.

There are, of course, limits to what one should do in case of an athletic injury. The basic responsibilities in providing first aid are:

1. To protect the individual from further harm.
2. To maintain life or attempt to restore life.
3. To comfort and reassure the individual.
4. To activate the emergency medical system.[42]

Do not try to do too much and change "first aid" to "worst aid." This happened in a roller skating case in New Jersey.[43] While skating, the plaintiff fell and sustained a fracture of her left arm. She was taken to the defendant's premises where an officer of the defendant corporation attempted to set her arm. He manipulated the plaintiff's factured arm and applied traction to it. When asked whether or not he was a doctor the officer replied in the negative, stating that as a prize-fight manager he had experience in such matters. The plaintiff charged the defendant with unlawfully attempting to set the arm and with commiting an assault and battery upon the plaintiff. It was further alleged that the defendant had no medical experience or capacity to treat the plaintiff and although the plaintiff requested the defendant to stop, the employee maliciously continued to mistreat her. A lower court sustained the defendant's motion to dismiss and the plaintiff appealed. The Superior Court held that the plaintiff's case should have been submitted to the jury on question of the defendant's liability for the alleged assault and battery.

In a California case, the plaintiff was tackled on a quarterback sneak during a preseason interschool scrimmage.[44] As he was falling forward another player fell on top of him. After this play the plaintiff lay on his back unable to get to his feet. The coach, suspecting a neck injury, had the player take hold of his hands to see if he could grip. The plaintiff was able to move his hands at that time. According to one witness, the injured player was then carried off of the field by eight boys, four on each side, with no one directing the movement. After the plaintiff was moved off the field to the sidelines, he was unable to move his hands, fingers, and feet. A physician testified it was his opinion that the plaintiff must have sustained additional damage to the spinal cord after being tackled, and that the removal of the plaintiff from the field without the use of a stretcher was an improper medical practice in view of the symptoms. The jury returned a verdict in favor of the plaintiff in the sum of $325,000.

Both of these cases involved the administration of treatment or movement of an injured party by officials who were not trained to treat or move participants with serious injuries. It is at such a time that a well-organized program of emergency medical care should operate and provide access to proper medical treatment. Teachers, coaches, athletic trainers, school administrators, school nurses, and physicians must all be involved in the development of such a program and be aware of the procedures necessary to carry out the program.

Based on patient examination procedures frequently used by emergency medical technicians and paramedics, the program shown in Figure 4-2 was adopted by Matthew T. Costello, Athletic Trainer at Plainfield (N.J.) High School.[45] It is to be used for evaluating an injured athlete, only by those who are adequately trained.

Fig. 4-2

STEPS	COMMENTS
Observe the scene and the position of the athlete. Is the athlete conscious or unconscious?	Check for any clues to the nature of the injury. If conscious, begin talking to the athlete. Identify yourself. Is there any pain? How did the injury occury. Never excite the athlete. Be tactful, calming and professional at all times.
Check the airway, breathing, circulation and obvious severe bleeding.	Be especially thorough if the athlete is unconscious.

* Reprinted with permission from Cramer Products' *The First Aider.* October, 1979.

STEPS	COMMENTS
Correct all life-threatening situations immediately.	Caution: always suspect a cervical injury after force injuries, particularly if a head injury is present. In these cases never hyperextend the neck to open the airway. Use the jaw thrust or chin lift method to produce an airway.
Observe for general deformity.	This can be brief, particularly for a conscious athlete. Caution: do not allow obvious injuries to prevent your discovering all injuries.
Begin body check.	Explain to the conscious athlete what you are about to do and ask him if he feels discomfort. Watch the athlete's face for signs of pain as you touch him. The unconscious or semiconscious athlete may flinch or groan when a sensitive area is touch.
Gently feel all 7 cervical vertebrae for tenderness or deformity without moving the athlete.	Deformity is rare.
Examine top of athlete's head and scalp for tenderness or deformity without moving the athlete.	Bumps or depression could incicate skull fracture. (Was patient unconscious for any amount of time?)
Examine the pupils.	Do pupils react to beam of flashlight? Are pupils unequal? Dilated? Pinpoint or constricted? Dull lusterless? Do both eyes focus and move together? (Caution: 17% of population have pupils unequal in size.)
Check for drainage of blood or cerebrospinal fluid from ears and nose.	Cerebrospinal fluid drainage indicates skull fracture. Caution: do not stop drainage.

STEPS	COMMENTS
Check shoulders, collarbone and ribs.	Caution: exert only enough pressure to determine if a fracture is present. Good judgment is needed during this entire procedure. Obviously, you need to apply less pressure on the collarbone than on the thigh. Never seek crepitus or grating. If the athlete complains of localized pain or if angulation is present, that body part need not be touched.
Check each arm, one at a time, from shoulder to hand. Have conscious athlete squeeze your hand.	Limbs must be examined separately. Otherwise, if a reaction occurs, the trainer will not know which limb is injured. For the same reason this exam is done by only one person. Use both hands around each limb opposite each other and with thumbs in line. Loss of ability to move or squeeze your hand, as well as numbness, tingling or loss of sensation should make you suspect a cervical spine injury.
Gently press upper and lower abdomen and the hips.	A rigid abdomen may mean injury to or inflammation of the abdomen.
Gently examine the rest of the spine.	However, don't move the athlete if you suspect a cervical spine injury.
Examine each leg separately— thigh, knee, lower leg and foot. Ask athlete to move his foot.	Loss of mobility of feet or legs as well as tingling, numbness or loss of sensation should make you suspect a spinal injury. Check legs with same hand technique as used on arms.

It is important that the trainer survey the athlete thoroughly. Initially, the trainer should treat only life-threatening situations. Care for all injuries by priority of need. Be aware of shock, check blood pressure, pulse, and respiration. Note the color of the patient's skin and nails. Finally know your athletes and any special medical problems they might have. These steps should *only* be used by adequately trained individuals. Whever one assumes the moral duty to aid an injured person, one also assumes the legal duty to aid them properly.

4.14 RECORDS AND RECORD-KEEPING

One does not regard record keeping as a supervisory duty and indeed it is not. It is however, a method of proving and planning and of obtaining pertinent data at the time of injury. In light of recent court cases, now is an appropriate time for teachers and coaches to review their record keeping skills, particularly in regards to plans of instruction, injury and accident reports, and storage of records. Occasionally, plans are referred to in court cases, such as in the *Keesee* case cited earlier, in which the teacher kept a plan book but apparently did not preserve it for use as evidence. Records indicating proper planning and the establishment of proper procedures are valuable evidence in the issue of foreseeability (what a reasonably careful and thoughtful person would expect and plan for at the time of an occurence and under the same circumstances—not hindsight).

Plans of instruction should indicate that the correct sequence and progression of activities were followed, that proper warm-ups took place prior to participation, and that consideration was given to safety while conducting the activity. The plans will contain other items as well, but these three elements are essential. A copy of these plans should be kept by the teacher. Plans of instruction also need constant revision to incorporate changes in instruction and improvements in technology. Formats for lesson plans and unit plans are present in most textbooks on teaching methods.

Standard accident report forms are also available, such as the one developed by the National Safety Council shown in Figure 4-3. As with instructional plans, the content of accident report forms is important. When filling out such a form, one should be descriptive but not judgmental. Teachers and coaches can observe, but they probably have not been trained to diagnose. The report form should thus contain observations, not pseudomedical evaluations.

Records, particularly those involving units of instruction, medical histories of students, and accident reports, should be stored and

Fig. 4-3.

STANDARD STUDENT ACCIDENT REPORT FORM.*

Part A. Information on ALL Accidents

1. Name: _____ Home Address: _____
2. School: _____ Sex: M☐: F☐: Age: ____ Grade or Classification: _____
3. Time accident occurred: Hour _____ A.M.: _____ P.M. Date: _____
4. Place of Accident: School Building ☐   School Grounds ☐   To or from School ☐   Home ☐   Elsewhere ☐

5. **NATURE OF INJURY**

Abrasion ____	Fracture ____	**DESCRIPTION OF THE ACCIDENT**
Amputation ____	Laceration ____	How did accident happen? What was student doing? Where was
Asphyxiation ____	Poisoning ____	student? List specifically unsafe acts and unsafe conditions existing.
Bite ____	Puncture ____	Specify any tool, machine or equipment involved. ____
Bruise ____	Scalds ____	
Burn ____	Scratches ____	
Concussion ____	Shock (el.) ____	
Cut ____	Sprain ____	
Dislocation ____		
Other (specify) ____		

PART OF BODY INJURED

Abdomen ____	Foot ____	
Ankle ____	Hand ____	
Arm ____	Head ____	
Back ____	Knee ____	
Chest ____	Leg ____	
Ear ____	Mouth ____	
Elbow ____	Nose ____	
Eye ____	Scalp ____	
Face ____	Tooth ____	
Finger ____	Wrist ____	
Other (specify) ____		

6. Degree of Injury: Death ☐   Permanent Impairment ☐   Temporary Disability ☐   Nondisabling ☐
7. Total number of days lost from school: _____ (To be filled in when student returns to school)

Part B. Additional Information on School Jurisdiction Accidents

8. Teacher in charge when accident occurred (Enter name): _____
Present at scene of accident: No: _____ Yes: _____

9. **IMMEDIATE ACTION TAKEN**
First-aid Treatment ____ By (Name): _____
Sent to School Nurse ____ By (Name): _____
Sent Home ____ By (Name): _____
Sent to Physician ____ By (Name): _____
Physician's Name: _____
Sent to Hospital ____ By (Name): _____
Name of Hospital: _____

10. Was a parent or other individual notified?   No: __ Yes: __ When: _____ How: _____
Name of individual notified: _____
By whom? (Enter name): _____
11. Witnesses: 1. Name: _____ Address: _____
2. Name: _____ Address: _____

12. **LOCATION**

	Specify Activity		Specify Activity	Remarks
Athletic field	_____	Locker	_____	What recommendations do you have for
Auditorium	_____	Pool	_____	preventing other accidents of this type?
Cafeteria	_____	Sch. Grounds	_____	
Classroom	_____	Shop	_____	
Corridor	_____	Showers	_____	
Dressing room	_____	Stairs	_____	
Gymnasium	_____	Toilets and		
Home Econ.	_____	Washrooms	_____	
Laboratories	_____	Other (specify)	_____	

Signed: Principal: _____ Teacher: _____

* Reprinted by permission of the National Safety Council.

should provide easily retrievable information. Storage time for such records is longer than many teachers and coaches realize. Depending on state law, a minor student has the right to bring lawsuit until two to three years after he reaches his majority. So that he may better defend his actions, it is possible that a teacher or coach may have to retrieve records ten or more years old.

4.15 SUMMARY

In summary, steps should be taken by a teacher or coach to reduce injury and also to reduce the likelihood of lawsuit in case of an injury. Teachers and coaches should:

1. Establish procedures for accidents and emergencies, including an appropriate set of forms. Safety rules and regulations should be included in these procedures, and enforced in the programs.

2. Establish an adequate plan of supervision that involves only competent personnel.

3. Regularly and thoroughly inspect facilities, apparatus, and equipment, and establish a program of preventive maintenance.

4. Set up activity programs based upon skill and experience, the appropriateness of the activity for the students, proper progression through the activity, and adequate safety and instructional practices.

5. In case of an injury, do not force first aid upon a person. Render only emergency first aid treatment. Call the nurse or physician immediately and notify parents. Take extreme care if the potential for injury to the spinal cord exists. If doubt exists, leave the injured in place until qualified personnel come to either treat or move the injured.

6. Complete records of the injury observations as soon as possible.

7. Initiate service education programs that include first aid and emergency procedures (especially for sport-specific injuries), safety awareness, and the development of safety procedures for physical education and athletic activities.

The National Collegiate Athletic Association Committee on Competetive Safeguards and Medical Aspects of Sports advocates the following sports safety guidelines:[46]

1. Preparticipation medical exam: Before an athlete accepts the rigors of organized sport, his/her health status should be evaluated. When the athlete first enters the college athletic program,

a thorough exam should be required. Subsequently, an annual health history update with use of referral exams when warranted is sufficient.

2. Health insurance: Each student-athlete should have or secure, by parental coverage or institutional plan, access to customary hospitalization and physician benefits for defraying the costs of a significant injury or illness.

3. Preseason preparation: Particular practices and controls should protect the candidate from premature exposure to the full rigors of the sport. Preseason conditioning recommendations will help the candidate arrive at the first practice at optimum readiness. Attention to heat stress and cautious matching of candidates during the first weeks are additional considerations.

4. Acceptance of risk: "Informed consent" or "waiver of responsibility" by athletes, or their parents if of minority age, should be based on an informed awareness of the risk of injury being accepted as a result of the student-athlete's participation in the sport involved. Not only does the individual share responsibility in preventive measures, but he or she should appreciate the nature and significance of these measures.

5. Planning and supervision: Competent attention to a sizable group of energetic and highly motivated student-athletes can only be attained by appropriate planning. Such planning should ensure both general supervision and organized instruction. Instruction should include individualized attention to the refinements of skill development and conditioning. In addition, first aid evaluations should be included with the instruction. Such planning for particular health and safety concerns should take into consideration conditions which are encountered during travel for competitive purposes as well.

6. Equipment: As a result of the increase in product liability litigation, purchasers of equipment should be aware of impending as well as current safety standards being recommended by authoritative groups and should utilize only known reputable dealers. In addition, attention should be directed to the proper repair and fitting of equipment.

7. Facility: The adequacy and conditions of the facilities used for particular activities should not be overlooked, and periodic examination of the facilities should be conducted. Inspection of the facilities should include not only the competitive area, but warm-up and adjacent areas.

8. Emergency care: Reasonable attention to all possible preventive measures will not eliminate sports injuries. Each scheduled session, practice or contest of an institution-sponsored sport therefore should have the following:

   The presence of immediate availability of a person qualified and delegated to render emergency care to a stricken participant.

   Planned access to a physician by phone or nearby presence for prompt medical evaluation of the situation when warranted.

   Planned access to a medical facility—including a plan for communication and transportation between the athletic site and medical facility—for prompt medical services when warranted.

   A thorough understanding by all affected parties, including the leadership of visiting teams, of the personnel and procedures involved.

9. Records: Documentation is fundamental to administration. authoritative sports safety regulations, standards, and guidelines kept current and on file provide ready reference and understanding. Waiver forms may not present lawsuits, but they help reflect organized attention to injury control.

Beyond these general suggestions, specific recommendations have been made for some sports. For example, the N.C.A.A. committee on Competitive Safeguards and Medical Aspects of Sports has the following recommendations for football coaches to develop a shared responsibility for safety with athletes in football:[47]

The committee encourages football coaches to discuss the following information with their squads, put it on each player's locker for emphasis, and then remind them of the essentials periodically during the season:

1. Serious head and neck injuries, leading to death, permanent brain damage, or quadriplegia (extensive paralysis from injury to the spinal cord at the neck level), occur each year in football. The toll is relatively small (less than one fatality for every 100,000 players and an estimated two to three non-fatal severe brain and spinal cord injuries for every 100,000 players), but persistent. They cannot be completely prevented due to the tremendous forces occasionally encountered in football collisions, but they can be minimized by manufacturer, coach and player compliance with accepted safety standards.

2. The NOCSAE seal on a helmet indicates that a manufacturer has complied with the best available engineering standards for head protection. By keeping a proper fit, by not modifying its design

and by reporting to the coach or equipment manager any need for its maintenance, the athlete is also complying with the purpose of the NOCSAE standard.

3. The rules against intentional butting, ramming, or spearing the opponent with the helmeted head are there to protect the helmeted person much more than the opponent being hit. No player shall intentionally strike a runner with the crown or the top of his helmet. The athlete who does not comply with these rules is the candidate for catastrophic injury. For example, no helmet can offer protection to the neck, and quadriplegia now occurs more frequently than brain damage. The typical scenario of this catastrophic injury in football is the lowering of one's head while making a tackle. The momentum of the body tries to bend the neck after the helmeted head is stopped by the impact, and the cervical spine cannot be "splinted" as well by the neck's muscles with the head lowered as it can with the preferred "face up, eyes forward, neck bulled" position. When the force at impact is sufficient, the vertebrae in the neck can dislocate or break, cause damage to the spinal cord they had been protecting and thereby produce permanent loss of motor and sensory function below the level of injury.

4. Because of the impact forces in football, even the face up position is no guarantee that that position can be maintained at the moment of impact. Consequently, the teaching of blocking/tackling techniques which keep the helmted head from receiving the brunt of the impact are now required by rule and coaching ethics, and coaching techniques which help athletes maintain or regain the "face up" position during the milieu of a play must be respected by the athletes.

This illustration covers only one significant safety problem in one sport. Other sports and other concerns within football can be similarly approached. The Committee on Competitive Safeguards and Medical Aspects of Sports recommends that coaches acquaint athletes with the risks of injury and the rules and practices that are being employed to minimize his/her risk of significant injury while pursuing the many benefits of sport. The athlete and the athletic program have a mutual need for an informed awareness of the risks being accepted and for sharing the responsibility for controlling those risks.

4.16 BALANCE FUN WITH SAFETY

It is important for teachers and coaches to reduce the danger of risk in an activity, especially risks not inherent in the activity, without removing the fun. If fun is eliminated, activities may turn out to be like the game described by David Ross.[48]

FOOTBALL ACCORDING TO LAW*

January 2, 1979. The University of Michigan filed suit in Los Angeles Superior Court for an order directing the Rose Bowl committee to alter the score of the 1979 Rose Bowl Game to 10-10; or, in the alternative, to order relpaying of the game after the controversial touchdown by USC's Charles White. Additional orders requested were; an injunction against the American Press and all coaches from causing a national football champion to be named until the final outcome of the suit; and order declaring that Charles White be compelled to testify as to what happened; the impounding of all video tapes and photographs of the controversial play.

On January 23, 1979, another suit, a class action, was brought against "Organized Crime, Inc." to restrain all bookmakers from paying off until the final outcome of the initial suit.

Simultaneously, several media organizations filed in Federal Court for an injunction against the impounding of all video tapes and photographs of the event on the grounds that it interfered with freedom of the press.

---

*Reprinted by permission of the *California State Bar Journal.* Copyright by the State Bar of California, 1979.

Alabama and Oklahoma Universities joined in the original suit, as did the ACLU, charging that football teams are entitled to due process.

Superior Court Judge Frank Kane, a UCLA alumnus, after hearing extensive arguments, granted the motion to replay the game. The motion was granted on September 9, 1979. Among Judge Kane's rulings:

1. The University of Michigan, contrary to the allegations of USC's lawyer, was properly incorporated in 1817. The evidentiary hearing on this issue took five weeks.
2. All bookmakers were ordered to withold payment on all bets. All persons who had already collected their bets were ordered to return them, with interest at 7%. Further, the judge refused the request of L.A. Police Department's attorney to obtain a list of the bookmakers. He ordered that portion of the file sealed. Media lawyers and the ACLU made no objections on "Freedom of the Press" grounds.
3. Charles White was ordered to give sworn testimoney, the judge ruling that there was no privilege against self-incrimination in a football game. Civil rights groups screamed racial prejudice.
4. All video tapes, photographs and audio recordings were ordered impounded. All parties were ordered to stop litigating in Federal Court and the Federal Court was ordered to mind its own Business. The judge authorized $200,000.00 of county funds to be spent by the Jet Propulsion Laboratory in analyzing the video tapes.

USC appealed the judge's ruling, alleging, among other things, that the trial judge was biased against USC. In Michigan's reply to the appeal, it was alleged that there was a conflict of interest in the game because a Michigan player was from the same hometown as a USC player and the two of them had played together on a high school sandlot team. Additionally, Michigan challenged the procedure used by the PAC 8 in becoming the PAC 10.

Again, after extensive evidentiary hearings, written and oral arguments and normal judicial procrastination, the Court of Appeal upheld the trial court's rulings, but expressed concern over the conflict of interest situation. Two of the three judges were UCLA alumni. The third was from Stanford.

The California Supreme Court felt that there were serious constitutional issues involved and ordered the entire matter transferred to them forthwith. That was March 20, 1980. Charles White, in the meantime, was playing for the Greenbay *(sic)* Packers and thereby was ineligible to replay the game. Several other players were also playing professional football. One starting lineman had died and two others were attending medical school. Their insurance prohibited them from using machinery or playing football. In discussing these problems, the Supreme Court remarked: "We cannot let the realities of the day interfere with the clear duties of this court." The matter was set for further argument and hearings on November 17, 1980.

Just before the California Supreme Court was to hear arguments on the matter, the U.S. Supreme Court issued a ruling in a similar case involving the intentional punching out of a professional basketball player. The issues were identical: the team of the "punchee" wanted to replay the game. In a terse opinion, the U.S. Supreme Court held: "As a matter of Constitutional Law, we don't think this court ought to waste its time on this drivel."

The attorneys for USC, citing the U.S. Supreme Court's opinion, sought a dismissal of the suit. In an equally terse opinion, the Chief Justice spoke for the California Court: "We believe that as a matter of independent California Constitutional Law the citizens and football players of this state are entitled to greater protection than that offered to U.S. citizens. The Rose Bowl is not drivel, it is important to the economy and psyche of a substantial portion of Californians."

In an unusual move the California Supreme Court en banc, called for a new evidentiary hearing on all issues in the case. The 430 lawyers representing each of the 197 parties to the hearing cried financial hardship. The court then ordered the state treasury to reimburse the attorneys for their fees. The order contained one sentence: "Justice knows not the bounds of cost."

The hearing was held in the Rose Bowl during the months of November and December 1980, and January through April 1981. Daily transcripts of the testimony were provided at state expense, to all parties and lawyers. All seven members of the court attended the hearings daily. (The 1981 Rose Bowl game, like that of 1980, was ordered suspended pending the outcome of the suit.) Normal court work was also suspended.

Mark Lane's allegation of two footballs on the field was extensively litigated, but, as the court said, was "substantially disproved" by the expects from the Jet Propulsion Laboratory. (No one raised the possibility of JPL's conflict of interest—what with being located in Pasadena and all.)

On May 2, 1981, the issue was finally fully submitted to the court. Hearings were reopened briefly during June to investigate the charge that there was conspiracy by the CIA to discredit the Rose

Bowl Committee. The charge was ruled "substantially untrue."

Finally, on July 17, 1981, the court, splitting 4 to 3, issued its ruling: A new game was ordered to be played. The insurance companies were ordered to provide insurance coverage for the two medical students, the NCAA was ordered to permit the professional ball players to be temporarily reclassified as amateur's (Jim Thorpe's heir's motion to include him were denied), and the brother of the deceased player was allowed to substitute in. A new Rose Parade was also ordered.

The game was played in the Rose Bowl on August 1, 1981. Of the 65,000 people attending the game, all but 275 were parties, lawyers, judges, clerks, secretaries, or some other way connected financially with the case (e.g., printers, messengers, copy machine salesmen, paper salesmen, etc.).

The game was played under modified rules. An isolated camera was focused on each player. At the end of each play, the video tapes were collected and brought to a special booth containing the monitors and the seven California Supreme Court Justices. Each play was dissected and analyzed, with both sides presenting arguments and testimony. The court then ruled on each play and the next play was executed on the field.

The game took 22 days to complete. The result, a scoreless tie. The 65,000 attendees had dwindled to 4.

As to the 4 remaining spectators left, one of them, a woman in a black robe, remarked that "Justice had finally been done." The other three nodded in approval.

The following day a new suit was filed. It seems that one Michigan lineman was attending USC Medical School. According to court records this was deemed a "blatant conflict of interest warranting a a complete new game."

NOTES

1. *Stanley v. Board of Education of the City of Chicago*, 9 Ill. App.3d 963, 293 N.E.2d 417 (1973).

2. *Styer v. Reading*, 360 PA 212, 61 A.2d 382 (1948).

3. Section 41-3-201, Montana Code Annotated.

4. "Regulation of Student Participation in Extracurricular Activites," A Legal Memorandum of the National Association of Secondary School Principals, Reston, Va., September, 1978.

5. *Darrin v. Gould*. 85 Wash.2d 859, 540 P.2d 882 (1975).

6. *Commonwealth, Packel v. Pennsylvania Intesch*. A.A., Pa. Cmnwlthl, 334 A.2d 839 (1974).

7. Herb Appenzeller and C. Thomas Ross, eds., "Sports and the Courts," 3 (Summer, 1980): 5-8.

8. Ibid.

9. Ibid. 189.

10. *Mokovich* v. *Independent School District No. 22*, 177 Minn. 446, 225 N.W. 292 (1929).

11. *Stevens* v. *Central Sch. Dist. No. 1 of Town of Tamapo*, 270 N.Y.S2d 23 (1966).

12. Neil J. Dougherty and Diane Bonanno., *Contemporary Approaches to the Teaching of Physical Education*. (Minneapolis. Burgess Publishing Company, 1979), p. 120.

13. *La Valley* v. *Stanford*, 70 N.Y.S.2d 460 (1947).

14. *De Gooyers* v *Harkness*, 70 S.D. 26, 13 N.W.2d 815 (1944).

15. *Rodriguez* v *Seattle School Dist. No. 1*, 66 Wash.2d 51, 401 P.2d 326 (1965).

16. *Bellman* v. *San Francisco High School District*, 11 Cal.2d 576, 81 P.2d 894 (1938).

17. *Keesee* v. *Board of Education of the City of New York*, 235 N.Y.S.2d 300 (1962).

18. *Brahatcek* v. *Millard School District No. 17*, 273 N.W.2d 680 (Nebraska, (1979).

19. *Summers* v. *Milwaukie Union High School District No. 5*. Or. App. 196, 481 P.2d 369 (1971).

20. *Kerby* v. *Elk Grove Union High School Dist.*, 1 Cal. App.2d 246, 36 P2d. 431 (1934).

21. *Vendrell* v. *School District No. 26C Malheur County*, 226 Ore. 263, 360 P.2d 282 (1961).

22. *Brooks* v. *Board of Education of City of New York*, 238 N.Y.S.2d 963, 189 N.E.2d 497 (1963).

23. *Pirkle* v. *Oakdale Union Grammar School Dist.*, 40 Cal.2d 207, 253 P.2d 1 (1953).

24. "Sports Injury Litigation." (Practising Law Institute Seminar, St. Francis Hotel, San Francisco, Ca., September 13-15, 1979). (New York: Practising Law Institute, 1979).

25. Ibid.

26. Ibid.

27. *Brackman* v. *Adrian*, 472 S.W.2d 735 (Tenn. 1971).

28. Betty van der Smissen, "Consideration of Legal Implications for Sponsoring Agencies and activity Leaders of Adventure Recreation Programs" (Lecture delivered at the A.A.L.R. Session of Legal Aspects of Risk Recreation, AAHPER National Convention, Kansas City, Mo., April 8, 1978).

29. "Sports Injury Litigation," supra.

30. *Jacques* v. *Lake Placid*, 332 N.Y.S.2d 743 (1972).

31. *Miller* v. *Cloidt and the Board of Education of the Borough of Chatham*, No. L 7241-62 (N.J. Super. 1964).

32. *Mogabgab* v. *Orleans Parish School Board*, La. App., 239 S2d 456 (1970).

33. Van der Smissen, "Consideration of Legal Implications for Sponsoring Agencies and Activity Leaders."

34. Ibid.

35. *Dailey* v. *Los Angeles Unified School Dist.* 84 Cal. Rptr. 325. vac. 87 Cal. Rptr. 376, 470 P.2d 360 (1970).

36. *Wright* v. *San Bernardino High School District*, 121 Cal. App.2d 342, 263 P.2d 25 (1953.).

37. *Cirillo* v. *City of Milwaukee.* 35 Wis.2d 705, 150 N.W.2d 460 (1967).

38. *Price* v. *Mt. Diablo Unified School District*, 177 Cal. App.2d 312, 2 Cal. Rptr. 23 (1960).

39. *Mark* v. *Colgate University*, 385 N.Y.S. 2d 621 (1976).

40. *Carabba* v. *Anacortes School District No. 103*, 72 Wash.2d 939, 435 P.2d 936 (1967).

41. *Nabozny* v. *Barnhill*, 31 Ill. App. 3d 212, 334 N.E.2d 258 (1975).

42. Pamela Bakhaus do Carmo and Angelo T. Patterson, *First Aid Principles and Procedures* (Englewood Cliffs, N.J.: Prentice Hall, 1976.) p.3.

43. *Clayton et al.* v. *New Dreamland Roller Skating Rink.* 14 N.J. Super. 390 (1951).

44. *Welch* v. *Dunsmuir Joint Union High School District*, 326 P.2d 633 (Cal. App. 1958).

45. Matthew T. Costello, "Evaluating an Injured Athlete: A Step-by-Step Procedure," *The First Aider*, 49, no. 2 (October 1979): 4, 13.

46. Available from the N.C.A.A. Committee on Competitive Safeguards and Medical Aspects of Sports, Nall Avenue at 63rd Street, P.O. Box 1906, Shawnee Mission, Kansas 66222.

47. N.C.A.A. Committee on Competitive Safeguards and Medical Aspects of Sport.

48. David Ross, "Football According to Law," *California State Bar Journal.* May/June 1979, pp. 170-171, Reprinted with permission from the *California State Bar Journal.*

5

MISCELLANEOUS MATTERS

While the allegation of negligence is the most common basis for a lawsuit in school athletics, there are other bases of which teachers and coaches should be aware. These include transportation, insurance, product liability, waivers, after-school activities, informed consent, and other populations such as officials and spectators.

5.1 TRANSPORTATION

The chances are quite good that at any given time, athletic teams somewhere are traveling to or from a contest. Sport is truly an international phenomenon, and all indications are that it will become even more so. The problems of travel have even created such special positions as traveling secretary for most professional athletic teams. Whether transporting students to the bowling alley for a physical education class, or transporting them to Tokyo for a collegiate football game, travel is a concern of today's teacher or coach.

The major concern is, of course, transporting students as safely as possible. In so doing, a number of options are available, including the choice of public, school, or private transportation. In each of these instances, there are a number of considerations to be made.

Perhaps the best way to travel in terms of reducing the liability of teachers and coaches is via public carrier. If this is available and affordable, it is the best means of transportation, provided the carrier is bonded. That is, the carrier must be capable, by means of a bond or insurance, of reimbursing you if a certain act is not carried out. Public carriers, especially those involved in interstate transportation, are also required to maintain their vehicles to higher specifications than individuals or school districts.

The most common means of transporting students for athletic events is through the use of school cars or school buses. The responsibility for maintaining these vehicles rests with the schools, as does the responsibility for hiring qualified drivers. This is undoubtedly the least expensive and most convenient method of transporting students. Unfortunately, as a matter of convenience, some drivers have questionable qualifications. Exmples of such drivers are students, trainers, and coaches who are driving such vehicles with inadequate insurance or improper licensure. If you are the driver of a school vehicle it may be necessary for you to have a chauffeur's license, and it may be necessary for you to have a carrier clause added to your own insurance, particularly if you are reimbursed for driving. A Montana statute, for example, states that "No person may drive any school bus transporting school children or any motor vehicle when in use for the transportation of persons for compensation until he has been licensed as a chauffeur for either such purpose and the license so indicates."[1]

Some schools purchase a form of "trip" insurance to cover drivers just for one trip. There are many different requirements and there are many different solutions, but the reasonable and prudent teacher or coach will discover what he must do to transport students safely.

Much of what was said regarding the use of school cars applies to the use of private cars for transporting students, especially if the owner is reimbursed. If a teacher's car is used to transport students, the car must be properly inspected and in satisfactory condition. If the teacher is the driver, he should have adequate and proper insurance. If the teacher or coach is being reimbursed with school funds for the use of the car, this may make him or her a carrier of sorts, with need of additional insurance.

In regards to reimbursement of drivers of private cars, the status of guest statutes and their applicability should be ascertained, because reimbursement may void such a statute. An example of a guest statute is:

> That no person who is transported by the owner or operator of a motor vehicle, as his guest, without payment for such transportation shall have a cause of action for damages against such owner or operator for injury, death or damage, unless such injury, death or damage shall have resulted from the gross and wonton negligence of the operation of such motor vehicle.[2]

In one such case, the court held that an automobile occupant was a guest although she was a high school cheerleader and was being transported to or from a school athletic event by a motorist who had been permitted by the school athletic director to transport cheerleaders without pay, instructions, or directions. Accordingly, a verdict was rendered in favor of the defendants.[3]

A driver of a car transporting students should be certain of coverage under a general automobile liability policy. The goal is to be protected against liability from the use of privately owned transportation by employees or nonemployees temporarily acting in the business of the school.

Another problem may arise with the use of student cars for transportation. Because of the nature of student cars and student drivers, this should be a last resort. A 1941 California case illustrates the problem.[4] For some years the teacher in charge of the tennis team had arranged with team students who had cars to take their teammates without cars home. The students were given a gallon of gasoline from the school pump for each ten miles traveled. One of the cars used for such transportation had been modified to what was called a "bug."

> It was equipped with special carburetor and a high compression head in order to give it more speed and power. It had no fenders, no running board, no top and ho horn. It had faulty lights, the speedometer was about twelve miles slow, the tires were worn and smooth, and the steering wheel was so loose that it was necessary to spin it a quarter of the way around before it took effect. The seat had been so lowered that the heads of the occupants came just above the doors, and when three people were in the front seat their knees stuck up so that it was practically impossible for the driver to reach the emergency brake. There is testimony that the brakes were faulty to the extent that when the car was traveling at high speeds "you might just as well not put them on."

On the way home from tennis practice, the car was involved in an accident, with one student killed and another seriously injured. The court held that the school district was liable for any negligence on the part of its employee in handling the school activity. Regardless of whether the teacher was authorized to provide transportation or not, if the teacher undertook to do so it was his duty to use such ordinary care as would a reasonably prudent person under the circumstances. The court held that the teacher should have known both of the condition of the car and of the driver's tendency to be reckless.

5.2 INSURANCE

Most states are now authorized to carry insurance to protect their employees ("save harmless laws) in case of a liability lawsuit. This is a practical example of the reduction of the umbrella defense of sovereign immunity. It is a good idea, whenever in doubt, to carry your own personal liability insurance. These coverages are available through numerous professional organizations. The American Alliance for Health, Physical Education, Recreation and Dance has such a policy available, at minimal cost. Phi Delta Kappa, the National Recreation and Park Association, the National Athletic Trainer Association, most educational associations, and many others provide similar insurance. Another inexpensive source of liability insurance is in the form of a "business pursuits" clause added to either a home owner's or renter's insurance policy. Such a clause should be an umbrella or unlimited clause covering the individual in all possible types of business or professional situations.

A teacher or coach should be familiar with the extent and limitations of insurance provided by the employer. This insurance should be a comprehensive public liability and property damage policy. Determine what the plan covers, to what extent, and under what conditions. To illustrate the latter point, assume that a teacher in a public school is giving private golf lessons after school and during the summer. This teacher should be sure to ascertain the limits on his or her school policy. Chances are any services rendered as a private contractor or professional are not covered by the school policy. Such "moonlighting" may require additional insurance. Low-cost liability insurance such as is offered by AAHPERD may also be unsatisfactory for such private employment, although it may be a good, cheap source of insurance for a teaching or coaching position. Similarly, a "business pursuits" clause added to one's home owner's or renter's policy, while another good, inexpensive way to obtain liability insurance for one's primary occupation, may not be adequate for extra, private employment. It is important that a physical educator or coach be concerned about liability insurance, and that he be adequately covered in all situations in which he is teaching or coaching.

When evaluating various insurance plans, a teacher or coach should consider the presence of limitations on notice, claim, or discovery periods. These may be loosely defined as that period of time after the lapse of coverage in which claim against the policy will still be honored by the carrier. Ideally, a policy will contain no such limitation, thereby enabling a teacher to be protected from a lawsuit brought by a student for an incident which has occurred in years past.

Additionally, the amount of the insurance coverage should not be minimal or nominal. A competent insurance agent or advisor should be consulted to assure that adequate coverage is provided for the potential exposure of the activities. Adequate coverage should not be substantially more expensive than basic insurance coverage.

It is also wise to insure program participants through a comprehensive health and accident insurance policy. These policies are generally in two forms: a group policy form that covers participants for almost all kinds of accidental injuries except those incurred while participating in athletics, and a policy covering participation in the exception, athletics. Most of these insurance plans are inadequate, and they do not relieve a teacher or coach of liability, but as Charles Bucher notes in *Administration of Physical Education and Athletic Programs:*

It is imperative for the various coaches to become aware of the insurance coverage so that when accidents do happen, they can inform the athletes of the proper procedure to follow in filing reports and claims. Usually the business office will supply policies for every participant in a covered athletic team. The coach should not only be knowledgeable, but he should also show concern for accident victims. This is not only a form of good public relations, but it may also make the difference in the parents' minds concerning a lawsuit. The coaches then must be instructed in the proper attitude to take when such mishaps occur.[5]

5.3 PRODUCT LIABILITY

although product liability cases involving teachers and coaches are not as numerous as negligence cases, teachers and coaches are listed as codefendants in about one-third of the product liability lawsuits involving physical eduction and athletic equipoment.[6] Involvement is possible, especially if a teacher or coach is connected with the manufacturing, selling, advertising, or representing of a product. Product liability is the liability of the manufacturer to the user of its products for personal injury or property damage resulting from the use of those products. Allegations usually made in product liability suits include:

1. defective construction or materials;
2. failure to comply with codes;
3. failure to investigate the sciences;
4. failure to properly warn the user of hazards;
5. failure of the product to perform as advertised;
6. improper design;
7. failure fault of two or more manufacturers.[7]

Interest in the topic of product liability by teachers and coaches is the result of several well-publicized cases, such as the recent $5.3 milion football helmet verdict. Some celebrities have also been charged with proving they used or tested a product prior to becoming a spokesman for that product, such as Bruce Jenner and the "Breakfast of Champions." While not technically product liability cases, such instances do emphasize the relationship between a spokesman and a product, and the need for a valid relationship.

A number of examples of product liability lawsuits in physical activities exist, usually against the manufacturer but frequently involving the coach or teacher. An out-of-court settlement was reached in a 1977 trampoline case.[8] In this case a student became paralyzed following a fall on a trampoline. She was attempting a double back somersault while wearing a spotting belt made by defendant-manufacturer. The lawsuit against the manufacturer was based on their failure to provide instructions in the use of the spotting belt. The plaintiff alleged that the defendant should have known that the belt would be dangerous unless the participant was reasonably and adequately informed of the danger and properly instructed in its use.

In a 1973 Washington case, the plaintiff was injured while attending a gymnastics class under the supervision of the local Y.M.C.A.[9] As she was exercising on the uneven parallel bars, the top bar separated from its saddles and she fell five to seven feet, landing on her back and sustaining injury. The court ruled that the burden of proof that the product was in a defective condition at the time it left the hands of the particular seller was upon the injured plaintiff. Since the record showed that the top bar was improperly fastened and therefore inadequate for the stress of an exercising body, the court concluded that there was no question of the inherent defective and dangerous condition of the apparatus at the time of injury. Further, the court found the apparatus was in the same dangerous and defective condition when it left the manufacturer's plant. A new trial was granted, with the only issue being the determination of damages.

From a stance of *caveat emptor,* "let the buyer beware," courts have evolved a number of theories for causes of action to injured consumers in a product liability case. These include:*

Warranties. Expressed or implied breach of a manufacturer's promise. Liability in warranty arrises when damage is caused by the failure of a product to measure up to the expressed or implied representation on the part of the manufacturer or supplier. The manufacturer of a perfectly made product can be liable if he has represented that the product will do something that it does not do.

Negligence. A manufacturer is liable for harm caused by the lawful use of a product in a manner and for a purpose for which it was manufactured, if the manufacturer has failed to exercise reasonable care in manufacturing the product. In particular, manufacturer negligence will be investigated in the areas of design, construction, inspection, testing, and warning.

Strict liability in tort. This theory imposes liability upon the manufacturer for any injury or destruction of property proximately caused by a defective product. The plaintiff must prove

---

* Reprinted by permission from Michel A. Coccia, John W. Dondanville, and Thomas R. Nelson, *Product Liability: Trends and Implications* (New York: American Management Association, Inc., 1970, page 14.

that the product was defective and unreasonably dangerous at the time it was manufactured. In addition, courts have charged a manufacturer with a duty to warn the user against any use of the product that could cause harm, if it is at all foreseeable to the manufacturer that such harm could result.

Since the emphasis above is on the manufacturer, product liability does not directly apply to teachers and coaches. It does indirectly, in the following ways:

1. As mentioned before, teachers or coaches are listed as code-fendants in about one-third of the products liability cases involving athletic equipment. Since the average length of time for the resolution of these large lawsuits is 69 months, they may have a long-term exposure to the stress and trauma of litigation.

2. The cost of product liability lawsuits is passed on to the consumers. Several athletic equipment manufacturers have stopped manufacturing football helmets because of lawsuits in this area. One estimate is that the cost of a football helmet may increase tenfold because of these lawsuits and the subsequent increase in insurance rates. There is a possibility that, due to the high injury rate, the severity of injury, and the resulting increase in the cost of the insurance, whole activities and sports, such as trampoline and football, may be threatened with extinction.

3. In some cases, the nature and techniques of a sport are caused to change. The American Society for Testing and Materials has a poster available for teaching trampoline, complete with warnings of the possible hazards and the recommendation of the United States Gymnastics Safety Association that:

   no somersaults be attempted in introductory physical education trampoline classes. When progression is made to somersaulting, it should be attempted only in a safety harness controlled by a certified instructor.[10]

   Two major organizations are involved in developing standards related to athletic equipment. These are the National Operations Committee on Standards for Athletic Equipment (NOCSAE) and the American Society for Testing and Materials (ASTM). As changes in the use of equipment occur, teachers and coaches must update their methodology to meet the new standards for equipment use. The same is true of new products. A teacher or coach must be aware of new and better protective equipment available in the activities they lead.

4. Manufacturers are endeavoring to meet the demands of the courts to do all that they can to produce a good product. This

places more of the burden on teachers and coaches to make sure that the product is used properly.

The flow chart in Figure 5-1 indicates what should be done by teachers and coaches to minimize the possibility of a product-related lawsuit.

Fig. 5-1.

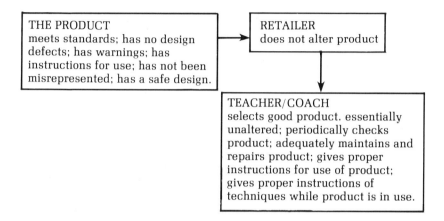

THE PRODUCT
meets standards; has no design defects; has warnings; has instructions for use; has not been misrepresented; has a safe design.

RETAILER
does not alter product

TEACHER/COACH
selects good product. essentially unaltered; periodically checks product; adequately maintains and repairs product; gives proper instructions for use of product; gives proper instructions of techniques while product is in use.

5.4 WAIVERS AND RELEASES

It is quite common for participants who are about to take part in an activity to sign a statement indicating that the sponsoring agency and its agents will be free from liability in case of an injury. In some cases, especially with minors, the parents are also asked to sign, thereby agreeing to the statement.

Such waivers seem to have little legal validity for avoiding lawsuit. There are several reasons for this. First, a waiver is regarded as a form of contract, and a minor cannot contract legally. A signed waiver by a minor is worthless, as he may still bring a lawsuit when he reaches his majority and is capable of such legal decisions. Further, even if a minor signs a waiver or release, his parents can still bring suit. If both the minor and the parents sign a waiver, the parents may relinquish the rights to recover damages, but they may not be able to waive negligence which injures the minor. A child may still be able to sue for pain and suffering, for medical bills and dimunition of earning capacity, and for loss of wages after he reaches full age.[11] A waiver will not release a teacher or coach from negligence, as teachers and coaches generally have the responsibility not to let a child involve himself in considerable risk.

A second objection to such waivers is that the presence of an agreement exempting a person from liability may tend to produce a lack of care. The person charged with the responsibility for administering a program, if he knows the opportunity for liability is waived, may not be as diligent in providing safe conditions for the program as he would if the potential for lawsuit did exist. A waiver cannot be used to produce a lower standard of care in regards to participants.

A final objection to the waiver is based simply on the legal opinion that no individual may contract against his own negligence. A waiver, in essence, would free one from liability for future actions, and since no one can predict future actions with great accuracy, any such contract is questionable and unwise.

In summary, waivers, releases, and parental permission slips should be used, but used as administrative procedure, and not as a protection from lawsuit. According to Van der Smissen, "the permits, however, are an excellent deterrent to parents bringing lawsuits and serve a very valuable public relations purpose.[12] But if negligence occurs, these waivers have little, if any, legal value.

Enough legal value, apparently, to encourage at least one state bar association to use a waiver. The following was used by the State Bar of Montana as sponsors of a "fun run" in 1981. It seems to be as good a model as any.

> RELEASE: In consideration of the acceptance of my entry, I for myself, my executors, administrators and assignees, hereby release and discharge the State Bar of Montana, Western Montana Bar Association, the race sponsors, their agents, employees, and all others associated with this event, from any and all claims for damages, actions, demands and injuries arising out of my participating in the event.
>
> I confirm and represent that I have full knowledge of the risks involved in this event and that I am physically fit and sufficiently trained to participate in it.

5.5 INFORMED CONSENT

There is at present increasing interest in a topic related to waivers and releases: informed consent. This is especially important in programs concerned with fitness testing and prescriptive exercises, as well as in the matter of research in physical education and sport. Indeed, any exercise testing involving human subjects must be concerned with obtaining the informed consent of participants prior to their participation.

To obtain informed consent, it is necessary to inform the participant of the techniques used in testing and the risks inherent in the testing procedure. Consent that is not informed is not consent. The possession of a signed consent form does not prevent lawsuit. Consent should be solicited, and obtained in written form, only after the participant thoroughly understands the risks involved in the testing techniques. Obtaining informed consent involves the following:

1. Inform the participant of the exercise program or testing procedures, with an explanation of the purpose of each. This explanation should be thorough and unbiased.

2. Inform the participant of the risks involved in the testing procedure along with a description of possible discomforts.

3. Inform the participant of the benefits expected for the testing procedure or exercise program.

4. Inform the participant of any alternative programs or tests that might be more advantageous for him or her.

5. Solicit questions regarding the testing procedures or exercise program and give unbiased answers to these inquiries.

6. Inform the participant that he or she is free at any time to withdraw consent and discontinue participation, without prejudice.

5.6 CONTRACTS FOR OFF-CAMPUS PROGRAMS

In order to provide a wider scope of activities and to overcome the limitations on physical education and athletic programs created by a lack of facilities or equipment, many schools are arranging for instruction or participation to take place off campus. As a result, some physical education curricula and perhaps some of the athletic program is conducted at or with an outside agency. Such an agency may be a bowling alley, golf course, ski area, riding academy, roller skating rink, dance school—any place that has special facilities for an activity. Even though the instruction will take place in an area not owned or leased by the school, those in charge of the school program maintain some degree of control and responsibility for the off-campus program. Activities frequently conducted on an off-campus basis include archery, bicycling, bowling, golf, hiking and camping, physical fitness, orienteering, aquatics, dance, handball, racquetball and squash, skiing, fishing, ice skating, roller skating, surfing, scuba diving, kayaking, canoeing, tennis—whatever the available facilities permit. It is expected that off-campus programs will increase both in popularity and in diversity of activities. The use of off-campus facilities, properly done, is an excellent means of increasing the scope of a physical education program.

All educational institutions have the responsibility to ensure that the off-campus program is valid. This was not the case in two well-publicized incidents in the fall of 1979. One of several problems at Arizona State University and the University of New Mexico involved credit given to athletes for classes they never attended and which were offered as off-campus classes by other institutions. Five New Mexico players stated they had no knowledge of how they became enrolled in the course and were unaware that they had received credit for it![13]

In addition to validity, schools also have the responsibility to review the off-campus programs so that the safety and welfare of students are protected. This degree of care should be:

> at least that degree of diligence in planning and conducting their off-campus programs that another group of reasonably prudent professionals would exercise in setting up a similar program in a similar situation.[14]

The care which schools are expected to exercise in establishing off-campus programs is roughly proportional to the amount of risk of injury involved in participating in a particular activity.[15] More care would be expected at a ski area than at a golf course.

At the off-campus site, instruction for the class may be given by the teacher or coach, may be under the supervision of the teacher or coach with specific instruction given by an agent of the off-campus program, or may be provided entirely by a specialist without the regular supervision of a faculty member. The latter arrangement is known as contracting. Regardless of the arrangement, the school is expected to use the degree of care that any group of reasonably prudent physical educators would use in establishing such a program. It is expected that the school would hire the best qualified instructor for the activity that they could afford, not just the teacher or coach, nor the owner of a private club. Whoever does teach the off-campus course must have expertise in the activity. This individual should have current certification, if appropriate. He should be able to communicate at the level of the students. Whoever teaches the activity must be able to do so within an understanding of the legal duties of a teacher or coach. These last two points may be very important if instruction is given by a person other than the school's teacher or coach.

5.7 GUIDELINES FOR CONTRACTING

Schools should contract with outside agencies so that the responsibility for liability is placed upon the agency and not the school. The agency will normally receive remuneration for its facilities, equipment, and instruction, and is therefore engaged in a proprietary function rather than the governmental function of education. If the school district and the outside agency act as partners in a joint endeavor, care must be taken to be certain that the school's insurance program is still valid. Any contract or letter of agreement between the school and the outside agency should include a statement identifying whose insurance is covering the students taking part in the off-campus program.[16] If the outside agency is to provide insurance, care should be taken to make sure there is adequate insurance provided, such as requiring a certificate of insurance that notes the school as a named insured. In this manner the school can be protected against a risk that may not be covered under its own policy.

Don E. Arnold suggests the following items be specified:

1. instructional sites and the dates and times of classes;
2. the amount and quality of any equipment needed and personal items of protective equipment to be provided;
3. the fee for use of the facility and the manner of its collection;
4. a description of the accident and general liability coverages such as the underwriter, agent, amount, dates of expiration, and procedures for filing claims.[17]

Another concept of contracting enables a program or activity to be taught not to a group but to individual students. This, of course, provides even more flexibility and diversity to a physical education program. It also requires specific consideration from the school beyond Arnold's guidelines.

The Bureau of Curriculum Services of the Pennsylvania Department of Education recommends the following guidelines for contracting:[18]

1. The contract method should receive approval from the local school directors. The contract should be a written agreement between the student, the physical education department and the administration.
2. Contracts should be written only for activities that are part of the planned course of study of the physical education department.

3. Contracts should contain performance objectives and descriptions of the planned experiences. They should include the equipment location, available resources, personnel, and expected outcomes for the student. Specific evaluation criteria should be stated.

4. Contracts should be developed, monitored and verified by a currently certified physical education instructor.

5. Contracts should be in writing, signed by the student, school district representative, and the parent or guardian, and should contain stipulations including: duration of contract, monitoring and counseling procedures, evaluation of student progress, estimated cost to student, insurance and liability coverage, travel considerations, equipment and materials required, and criteria for grading.

5.8 UNSUPERVISED USE OF A FACILITY

Teachers, coaches, and others who have access to the school gymnasium are frequently requested to allow various groups to use the gymnasium for recreation. In some instances this involves a rental fee and is done through guidelines established by the school board for such rentals. Sometimes, however, no fee is involved and a group of individuals simply wish to use the unsupervised gymnasium to exercise. This is especially common in small towns in which the gymnasium may be the only facility available for exercise, particularly during inclement weather.

It would be expensive for the school to hire a supervisor for all hours, such as during the Christmas vacation, and consequently the gymnasium is used with no supervisor present. In such a circumstance, the people who are exercising are licensees, that is, they have permission to enter and use the gymnasium but have not been invited to do so. The general rule regarding a safe place for licensees is that the area must be free of major hazards, particularly those that cannot be easily seen or ascertained, and the licensees must have been told of any changed conditions in the facility since their last visit. If the property is maintained in a safe condition, and if the licensees are warned of unobtrusive or changed conditions that may be hazardous, such "free play" may be allowed. This is stated with reservation. Unsupervised use of a physical education or athletic facility is usually desired by the community, but continues to be risky. A school policy regarding such use should be developed.

Injuries do occur, as the experience of an Idaho school district illustrates. During the Christmas holiday of 1967, six local boys drove to the high school gymnasium in a small Idaho community with the intention of playing an informal basketball game.[19] Upon arrival, they found the entrance locked. The boys were able to persuade the custodian to open the door and let them use the basketball court. After so doing, the custodian continued his cleaning duties. The plaintiff cleaned the playing surface of the gymnasium by sweeping the court with a wide dust mop or broom for five or ten minutes, while his friends changed clothes. The boys then began shooting baskets, using two worn leather basketballs which they found lying about the equipment room. Plaintiff was wearing basketball shoes and slacks. He was a member of the high school basketball team and an accomplished athlete. At least one of the other boys was a teammate of his on the school basketball teams. The boys split into two teams and played a "half-court" basketball game. Sometime during their play a shot came off the backboard and headed towards the out-of-bounds area. Plaintiff and opposing player ran for the loose ball, collided, and the plaintiff suffered a fracture in the cervical area of his spine. The plaintiff alleged that the lack of supervision, the use of an old ball, and the dirty floor were causative factors in the injury. The school district admitted that the custodian disregarded a policy of the school by permitting the boys to use the gymnasium, but claimed that the lack of supervision was not the cause of the accident, and that neither the physical conditions of the court nor the old basketball were legally causative of the injury. The school district was granted a summary judgment which was upheld on appeal. In commenting on the case the court summarized the situation of unsupervised play as follows:

> Generally, schools owe a duty to supervise the activities of their students whether they be engaged in curricular activities or non-required but school sponsored extra-curricular activities. . . .
> Further, a school must exercise ordinary care to keep its premises and facilities in reasonable safe condition for the use of minors who foreseeably will make use of the premises and facilities. . . .
> However, we offer no opinion on the question of whether schools must provide supervision under the circumstances before us for reasons stated here-after.
> On the claim that the school district breached its duty to supervise the boys' game, the record lacks any evidence as to how the presence of a coach or teacher would have prevented the collision of the boys chasing the rebounding basketball. . . .
> Physical contact in such a situation is an athletic contest is

foreseeable and expected. The general rule is that participants in an athletic contest accept the normal physical contact of the particular sport.

This decision is consistent with most, which maintain that schools do not owe students supervision for injuries that occur in a nonschool program. Schools are not expected to provide supervision during off-school hours for those programs that are not a part of the regular school program, but they must keep an area free from hazards or close the area.

5.9 OTHER POPULATIONS

One need only be a consistent reader of the sports page to become aware of the variety of legal issues now surfacing in sport. Most of the discussion in this text has centered on teachers and coaches and their professional relationships with students during a legal issue. Other "populations" are involved in such lawsuits, and some of these cases shed more light on the legal duties of a teacher or coach. For this discussion of tort liability, it is helpful to focus on two other sport populations that have been involved in lawsuits: spectators and officials.

Spectators

Spectators at a sporting event assume the normal risks of the game, whether they are in the bleachers or standing along the sidelines. As with players, this includes only those risks that are an inherent part of the activity. Thus unsafe or collapsing bleachers, or inadequate attempts by a school to keep spectators from crowding too close to a sideline and thus exposing themselves to the risk of contact from the play of the game are examples of actions for which a school or school official may be liable. It is expected that when one attends a baseball game there is some chance that one will have to fend off or catch a ball fouled into the stands. This ball should not, however, come through a hole in a protective screen. In The Natural, the hero vents his fury against a nagging fan by intentionally bombarding him with foul balls.[20] This would not be a normal consequence of the game of baseball, nor would any physical attack on a fan by a player.

A duty may be owed a spectator to provide him with a safe environment for watching a game.[21] This duty does not extend to spectators who choose to move away from the protected area for a closer or better look. In a Washington case, a sixty-seven-year-old grandmother, who had previously attended only one football game, was injured when a play ran over the sideline into the spectators standing at the fifty-yard line.[22] Bleachers were provided for the spectators but the grandmother and her daughter chose to stand nearer the field. The court held that risks apparent to an ordinary and prudent person are assumed, notwithstanding the admitted ignorance of the grandmother about football.

Officials

Just as Diogenes wandered through the streets in search of an honest man, coaches, administrators, and especially spectators are constantly in search of good officials. The problem is the definition of good. Like love, momentum and "good vibes," a good official belies precise definition. The standard of care for a game official is the same standard applied to teachers and coaches, that is, an official should behave as a reasonable and prudent qualified game official would under the circumstances.

This has been an issue in several court cases. In one instance, a group of Washington Redskins fans attempted to get the courts to overturn an official's decision that had cost their beloved Redskins a victory. This was dismissed as frivolous. A more significant type of action is illustrated by a 1968 Washington case involving high school wrestlers.[24] During the course of their deliberations in this case the jury requested an additional instruction regarding the standard of care applicable to the referee of this wrestling match. The referee was charged with negligence because a paralyzing injury occurred while his attention was diverted from the match. In one of the instructions to the jury, the judge set forth the following relationship between the school district and the official's behavior.

> The defendant school districts owed a duty to the student participants in the wrestling match to exercise reasonable and ordinary care to protect them from injury during the wrestling match. Under the evidence in this case, the only person who was carrying out his duty of the defendants was the referee, Robert Erhart. Accordingly, the question of whether or not the defendant school districts were negligent is narrowed down to a question of whether or not the referee, Robert Erhart, was negligent during the course of the wrestling match. If you find that the referee was negligent, then the school district defendants were negligent. If you find that the referee was not negligent, then the school district defendants were not negligent.

Erhardt was judged by the standard of care of the ordinarily prudent referee, not the ordinarily prudent man. The above instruction to the jury, upon appeal, was held to be proper. Game officials appear to be agents of the schools or organizations who hire them, and must meet the standard of care of a reasonable and prudent official.

5.10 PLAYER V. PLAYER LAWSUITS

As mentioned earlier, very few lawsuits allege negligence on the part of a fellow-competitor. In one case that did, a soccer case in which one player was kicked in the head by another, the court ruled that under standard rules of play, with adequate coaching and officiating, a player is charged with a legal duty to every other player on the field to refrain from conduct proscribed by a safety rule.[25] The court further stated that a player is liable for injury in a tort action if his conduct is such that it is either deliberate, willful, or with a reckless disregard for the safety of the other player so as to cause injury to that player.

Another player v. player case resulted from a collision in a softball game.[26] In this case, the defendant, who had been on first base, ran at full speed into the second baseman, hitting him under the chin with his left arm to keep him from executing a double play. The court acknowledged that while the second baseman may have assumed the risk of being spiked by a player sliding into second base, he did not assume the risk of the runner going out of his way to collide with him at full speed at a point five feet from the base. The court held that a participant assumes risks which are obvious and foreseeable, but not those risks resulting from the unexpected and unsportsmanlike conduct of fellow players. Recently, the 10th U.S. Circuit Court of Appeals (and subsequent Supreme Court Action) found that the intentional infliction of an injury by one player upon another can give rise to tort libability.[27] This was the opinion in a lawsuit involving an injury resulting from the player striking another with his forearm in the back of the head, while the injured player was kneeling on the ground with his back to the offender.

5.11 A THREAT TO SPORT?

One additional problem merits consideration. This is the possibility of a sport becoming so violent or so risky that its structure and existence is in jeopardy. While this may be extreme it could happen — in the minds of some it is happening. In *The Death of an American Game* John Underwood illustrates that the violence (particularly the intentional violence), the injury rate, and the subsequent litigation pose a threat to the nature and existence of football:*

---

* Reprinted by permission from John Underwood, *The Death of An American Game.* (Boston: Little Brown, 1979), pp. 13 and 16.

Most civilized social orders, even including the National Football League, will, in time, come to grips with a continuum of mindless violence and deal with it, provided it is ugly enough and of no lasting financial value. Football's natural roughness naturally spawns some over-the-line bullying, and you can even excuse some of it. This, however, is the brute face of spreading barbarism that would not have blended into the fabric of play were it it not for the greater outrage: the game's insane tolerance for its growing injury rate.

"The fallout," I said, "could be lethal."

"What fallout?"

"The most noxious kind. The kind that is dragging football into the courts with increasing frequency. The sport is crawling with lawyers."

Coaches, players, owners, and officials were in fact, going round and round in legal battles, contesting everything from breached contracts to slander. . . . Players, teenagers and adults—were suing over their broken bodies. Some were doing it from wheelchairs. Entire programs were being threatened with litigation. Manufacturers of the game's equipment were learning the meaning of judgment day.[28]

After citing several sample lawsuits, Underwood points out that as a result of the death of a high school football player the state of California had been pressured by schools and parents to make mandatory the attendance of a physician and an ambulance at every high school game, possibly as many as 1,500 games a week. As a result of these factors, Underwood asks:

1. If the cost of indemnifying a high school sport against the threat of litigation eliminates that sport, what happens to college sport? And, down the line, to pro-sport?

2. More ominously, if you have reached a point where an ambulance and a physician are needed at fieldside every time two teams go out to play, is it a sport?[29]

NOTES

1. Section 61-5-112. Montana Code Annotated.

2. *Kitzel* v. *Atkeson et al.,* 173 Kan. 198, 245 P.2d 170 (1952).

3. *Fessenden* v. *Smith*, 255 Iowa 1170, 124 N.W.2d 554 (1964).

4. *Hanson et al.* v. *Reedley Joint Union High School Dist. et al.* 43 Ca. 2d 643, 111 P.2d 415 (1941).

5. Charles Bucher, *Administration of Physical Education and Athletic Programs,* 7th ed. (St. Louis: C.V. Mosby, 1979), p. 440.

6. Don E. Arnold, "Sports Product Liability": JOPER November-December 1978, pp. 25-28.

7. Irwin Gray et al., *Product Liability: A Management Response* (New York: American Management Association, 1975), p. 4.

8. *Olson v. Nissen Corp.*, Iowa Linn County District Court, L.A. 1284, June 15, 1977.

9. *Curtiss v. Young Men's Christian Association of the Lower Columbia Basin.* 82 Wash.2d 455, 511 P.2d 991 (Wash. 1973).

10. Available from American Society for Testing and Materials, 1916 Race Street, Philadelphia, Pa. 19103. Also from United States Gymnastics Safety Association, Box 17241, Dulles International Airport, Washington, D.C. 20041.

11. Herb Appenzeller, *Physical Education and the Law* (Charlottesville, Va.: The Michie Company, 1978), p. 149.

12. Betty Van der Smissen, *Legal Liability of Cities and Schools for Injuries in Recreation and Parks* (Cincinnati: W.H. Anderson Co., 1968), p. 96.

13. John Papanek, "New Mexico: More Tremors", *Sports Illustrated.* December 17, 1979, pp. 75-76.

14. Don E. Arnold, "Legal Aspects of Off-Campus Physical Education Programs," JOPER, April 1979, pp 21-23.

15. Ibid.

16. Ibid.

17. Ibid.

18. *Contracting: An Approach to Providing Flexibility in the Physical Education Program.* Bureau of Curricular Service, Pennsylvania Dept. of Education, 1974. pp. 39-40.

19. *Albers v. Independent Sch. Dist. No. 302 of Lewis Co..* 94 Idaho 342, 487 P.2d 936 (1971).

20. Bernard Malamud, *The Natural* (New York: Farrar, Strauss and Giroux, 1961).

21. Van der Smissen, *Legal Liabilities of Cities and Schools.* p. 211.

22. *Perry v. Seattle Sch. Dist. No. 1* 66 Wash.2d 800, 405 P. 2d 589 (1965).

23. Van der Smissen, *Legal Liabilities of Cities and Schools.* p. 213.

24. *Carabba v. Anacortes School District No. 113.* 72 Wash.2d 939, 435 P.2d 936 (1968).

25. *Nabozny v. Barnhill.* 311 Ill. App.3d 212, 334 N.E.2d 258, (1975).

26. *Bourque v. Duplechin.* 331 S.2d 40 (La. App. 1976).

27. Robert G. Woolf, "Courts Coming Down Hard on Excessively Violent Players," *The National Law Journal.* January 7, 1980, p. 20.

28. John Underwood, *The Death of an American Game.* (Boston: Little Brown, 1979), p. 13.

29. Ibid. p. 16.

APPENDICES

APPENDIX A
Women and Sports: A Summary of Major Court Cases*

Name and Citation

HOLLANDER V. CONNECTICUT CONFERENCE, INC. NO. 11 49 27 (no reported decision)

Date March 29, 1971

Court and Judge

Superior Court New Haven County Connecticut, J. John C. Fitzgerald

Issue and Nature

Susan Hollander wanted to run on the boys' high school cross-country team, but was thrown off the team due to CIAC rules. No team for girls. Individual suit. Later settled by agreement with U.S. District Judge Newman (U.S.D.C. D Conn.). CIAA (Conn. Intercollegiate Athletic Association) will amend its regulations to permit girls to compete in non-contact sports in cases where no teams exist for girls.

Ruling and Statute

LOST. In favor of defendants. 14th Amendment, Equal Protection Consent decree issued on Jan. 16, 1973 to integrate all non-contact sports in Conn.

Notes of Interest

One of the first cases litigated. Cited physical safeguard for girls and removal of incentive and challenge to win for boys. "Athletic competition builds character in our boys. We do not need that kind of character in our girls, the women of tomorrow."

Name and Citation

GREGORIA V. BOARD OF EDUCATION OF ASBURY PARK (NEW JERSEY) NO. A-1227-70 Appellate Division

Date April 5, 1971

Court and Judge

Superior Court New Jersey

Issue and Nature

Female wanted to participate on boys' tennis team. No team for girls.

Ruling and Statute

LOST. In favor of defendants.

---

* "In The Running", Spring, 1981. Published by SPRINT, a national clearinghouse on information on sex equity in sports, 805 Fifteenth Street, Suite 822, Wshington D.C. 20005. Toll-free number: (800) 424-5162. SPRINT is a project of the Women's Equity Action League (WEAL), a non-profit national women's organization that seeks to secure legal and economic rights for women. List of cases compiled by Abigail Jones and Toni Clarke under the auspices of a grant from the Ford Foundation.

Notes of Interest
Appeals dismissed. Court did not find earlier (lower) court's decision that psychological well-being of girls is rational reason for exclusion to be unreasonable or arbitrary.

Name and Citation
REED V. NEBRASKA SCHOOL ACTIVITIES ASSOCIATION 341 Fed. Supp. 258 (D. Neb. 1972).

Date April 12, 1972

Court and Judge
U.S.D.C. D. Neb.

Issue and Nature
Debbie Reed wanted to play on boys' golf team. No team for girls. Argued the prohibiting Neb. Athletic Assocition Rule was a denial of her rights under the 14th Amendment. Individual suit.

Ruling and Statute
Won. Preliminary injunction granted.

Notes of Interest
Granted injunction allowing girls to participate. "If the program is valuable for boys, is it of no value for girls?

Name and Citation
HARRIS V. ILLINOIS HIGH SCHOOL ASSOCIATION. NO. S-Civ. 72-25

Date April 17, 1972

Court and Judge
U.S.D.C. S.D. Illinois

Issue and Nature
High School girl wanted to participate on varsity boys' tennis team. None for girls. Individual suit.

Ruling and Statute
Lost. In favor of defendants.

Notes of Interest
Court said that there is no "right" to participate in interscholastic competition. Classification by gender is "perfectly rational.

Name and Citation
BRENDEN V. INDEPENDENT SCHOOL DISTRICT. 342 Fed. Supp. 1224 (D. Minn. 1972) affirmed 477 F. 2nd 1292 (8th Cir. 1973)

Date May 1, 1972
April 18, 1973

Court and Judge
U.S.D.C. D. Minnesota J. Miles W. Lord
U.S. Ct. of Appeals 8th Circuit Judge Heaney

Issue and Nature
Antoinette St. Pierre & Peggy Brenden wanted to be on boys' cross-country, skiing, running, and tennis (respectively) teams. These two exceptionally skilled females were prohibited from participation with males in high school interscholastic athletics. No teams for girls.

Ruling and Statute
Won. In favor of girls. 41 USC 1983 (Civil Rights Act), Equal Protection Clause, 14th Amend. Appeals affirmed District Court decision. But explicitly confined ruling to non-contact.

Notes of Interest
Most significant athletics case decided under 14th Amend. Has been cited more frequently than any other case of its kind. Prohibiting rule was found invalid even under rational basis standard. Though not decided under Title IX, Court cited statute as new rational policy against discrimination in education. Thus, Brenden may provide foundation on which first cases under Title IX will be built.

Name and Citation
BUCHA V. ILLINOIS HIGH SCHOOL ASSOCIATION. 351 Fed. Supp. 69 (N.D. Ill. 1972)

Date Nov. 15, 1972

Court and Judge
U.S.D.C. N.D. Illinois Judge Austin

Issue and Nature
Sandra Lynn Bucha and friend (2 high school students) wanted to be on boys' swim team. Objected to by-laws of Illinois High school Association which applied restrictions to girls which were not applied to boys' sports program. Class Action.

Ruling and Statute
Lost. In favor of defendants. Constitution (no violation found).

Note of Interest
Neither Illinois nor U.S. had enacted legislation prohibiting sex discrimination in H.S. athletics. First separate but equal ruling. Girls program did exist and upheld on evidence of male superiority.

Name and Citation
HAAS V. SOUTH BEND COMMUNITY SCHOOL CORP. (Indiana H.S. Ath. Assoc.) 289 N.E. 2nd 495 (1972)

Date Nov. 27, 1972

Court and Judge
Superior Court of Indiana, Judge Hunter

Issue and Nature
Johnell Haas had qualified but was not permitted to join boys' golf team because of Indiana High School Athletic Assoc. rule. At the time, no girls' team.

Ruling and Statute
Won. In favor of girl. U.S.C.A. 14th Amendment

Notes of Interest
First decision by Appellate Court in any jurisdiction dealing with mixed

competition. "Until girls' programs comparable to those maintained for boys exist, the difference in athletic ability alone is not justification for the rule denying 'mixed' participation in non-contact sports."

Name and Citation
MORRIS V. MICHIGAN BOARD OF EDUCATION. 472 F.2nd 1207 (6th Circuit 1973)

Date Jan. 25, 1973

Court and Judge
U.S. Court of Appeals 6th Circuit Judge Edwards

Issue and Nature
Cynthia Morris and friend wanted to be on boys' tennis team. Individual suit. Girls team existed. Preliminary Injunction granted on April 27, 1972.

Ruling and Statute
Won. But changed injunction to apply to *non-contact* sports. Mich. Act no. 138 of Public Acts of 1972 passed after preliminary injunction, allowing females in all non-contact sports.

Note of Interest
Second Case permitting girls on boys team where girls team present.

Court and Judge
RITTACCO V. NORWIN SCHOOL DISTRICT. 361 F. Supp. 930 (W.D. Pa. 1973)

Date Aug. 3, 1973

Issue and Nature
U.S.D.C. W.D. Pennsylvania Judge Gourley

Issue and Nature
Roxanne Rittacco wanted to try out for boys' tennis team rather than girls' tennis team. Class Action. Challenged Athletic Assoc. rule.

Ruling and Statute
Lost. In favor of defendants. 14th Amendment.

Notes of Interest
Second Separate but Equal Ruling. Court made three points:)1 Rule did not unfairly discriminate; 2) girl had graduated and was no longer member of class; and 3) evidence proved girls' team developed better when sexes were segregated.

Name and Citation
NOW, ESSEX COUNTY CHAPTER V. LITTLE LEAGUE BASEBALL, INC. 127 N.J. Super. 522, 318 A. 2nd 33 (1974)

Date March 29, 1974

Court and Judge
New Jersey Superior Court Judge Confored

Issue and Nature
Essex County NOW filed for 8-12 year old girls who sought to play Little League baseball. Complained violation of NJ law against discrimination.

Ruling and Statute
Won. Ordered Little League Baseball, Inc. to admit girls to participate. NJ SA 10.3-1

Notes of Interest
Judge held girls of this age are not subjected to greater hazard of injury while playing ball than boys of same age.

Name and Citation
GILPIN V. KANSAS STATE HIGH SCHOOL ACTIVITIES ASSOCIATION, INC. 377 F. Supp. 1233 (D. Kan. 1974)

Date May 22, 1974

Court and Judge
U.S.D.C. D. Kansas Judge Theis

Issue and Nature
Tammie S. Gilpin, a junior at Wichita High School, wanted to be on a cross-country team. Individual suit. No team for girls.

Ruling and Statute
Won. In favor of Girl. 14th Amendment. 28 U.S.C. 1343; 42 U.S.C. 1983

Notes of Interest
Court implied ruling would have been otherwise had a separate team existed for girls. Sex-based classifications are subject to close scrutiny by courts under equal protection clause. Once again, court reinforced Separate but Equal.

Name and Citation
KING V. LITTLE LEAGUE BASEBALL, INC. 505 F.2nd 264 (6th Cir. 1974)

Date   Oct. 30, 1974

Court and Judge
U.S. Court of Appeals 6th Circuit Judge Engle

Issue and Nature
Carol Ann King wanted to be on the Little League Baseball team the "Orioles." She made the team based on ability but was dropped so the team's charter would not be revoked. No girls Little League team in Ypsilanti, MI area.

Ruling and Statute
Dismissed. For lack of subject matter jurisdiction. 5 & 14th Amends. 42 USC 1983. Dept. of Parks later resolved to allow girls to compete.

Notes of Interest
Judge held that complainant failed to state claim for relief on theory of sex discrimination.

Name and Citation
CLINTON V. NAGY 411 Fed. Supp. 1396 (N.D. Ohio 1974)

Date Nov. 14, 1974

Court and Judge
U.S.D.C., N.D. Ohio Judge Lambros

Issue and Nature
12 year old Brenda Clinton wanted to play in the Cleveland City recreation league on Cleveland Browns Muny Football teams. Claimed city regulation did not bear a relationship to any state purpose. Neither mother nor coach had any objection—she was prohibited solely because she was a girl.

Ruling and Statute
Won. In favor of girl. 14th Amendment. 42 U.S.C. 1983.

Notes of Interest
Age of team may limit applicability.

Name and Citation
FORTIN V. DARLINGTON LITTLE LEAGUE 376 F. Supp. 473 (D. RI., 1974) rev'd 514 F2nd 344 (1st Cir. 1975)

Date May 15, 1974; May 31, 1975

Court and Judge
U.S.D.C. D. Rhode Island; U.S. Court of Apeals 1st Circuit

Issue and Nature
10 year old Allison "pookie" Fortin claimed that she was denied the opportunity to try out because she was female—and that she was otherwise qualified. Plaintiff alleged the baseball park areas were public facilities and that community girls should not be denied opportunity to try out solely on sex.

Ruling and Statute
Won. In Favor of Girl. Reversed earlier District Court decision which was in favor of defendants.

Notes of Interest
Challenges organization's policy of prohibiting females on ground that physical differences between sexes would result in injury to girls.

Name and Citation
MAGILL V. AVONWORTH BASEBALL CONF., 516 F.2nd 1328 (3rd Cir., 1975)

Date May 8, 1975

Court and Judge
U.S. Ct. of Appeals 3rd Circuit Judge Aldisert

Issue and Nature
Challenge to allow 10 year old Pamela Magill to participate in Little League Baseball which used publicly owned baseball fields. Plaintiff sought injunction.

Ruling and Statute
Lost. In favor of defendants. Affirmed similar lower court. 14th Amendment, 42 USC. 1983, 1985

Notes of Interest
Court concluded plaintiff had failed to show significant state involvement in the baseball conference's discrimination.

Name and Citation

COMMONWEALTH V. PENNSYLVANIA INTERSCHOLASTIC ATHLETIC ASSOCIATION, Pa Commonwelath Ct., 334 A2d 839 (1975)

Date March 19, 1975

Court and Judge

Commonwealth Court of PA

Issue and Nature

Commonwealth filed suit against athletic association maintaining rule forbidding mixed competition was unconstitutional.

Ruling and Statute

Won. In favor of plaintiff. Rule declared unconstitutional. PA State ERA.

Notes of Interest

Opened contact as well as non-contact. Rejected physical differences and safety arguments. Although plaintiff did not seek relief for discrimination in football and wrestling, the court included these in its motion for summary judgment.

Name and Citation

LAVIN V. CHICAGO BOARD OF EDUCATION, 73 F.R.D. 438 (1975) LAVIN V. ILLINOIS HIGH SCHOOL ASSOCIATION, 527 F2d 58 (7th Cir. 1977)

Date Aug. 29, 1975; Jan. 17, 1977

Court and Judge

U.S.D.C. N.D. Ill.; U.S. Court of Appeals 7th Circuit

Issue and Nature

Lavin, female athlete, brought a Class Action covering all varsity interscholastic and intramural sports programs in the Chicago Public School system to allow girls to play on boys' teams. She had previously been denied the opportunity to play on the varsity baseball team because the H.S.A.A.'s by-laws said she couldn't. She sought declaratory and monetary relief.

Ruling and Statute

Won. In favor of girl. Reversed earlier District Ct. decision in which the plaintiff won money damages, but lost Class Action. Won Class Action in Ct. of Appeals. 14th Amendment, Equal Protection.

Notes of Interest

District Court awarded money damages and not class action because case should have been moot since girl had graduated. Ct. of Appeals overturned refusal to grant Class Action.

Name and Citation

DARRIN V. GOULD 540 P.2d. 882 (1975)

Date

Sep. 25, 1975

Court and Judge

Supreme Court of Washington Judge Charles Horowitz

Issue and Nature

Two well-qualified Darrin girls wanted to play on the high school football team. Carol, 16 years old, 5'6", and Delores, 14 years old, 5'9", 212 lbs., were barred from team because of "lighter bone structure!" Challenged state athletic association's rule which excluded girls. No girls' team present. Class Action. Girls had approval of parents and coach.

Ruling and Statute
Won. In favor of girls. Supreme Ct. reversed lower court ruling. State ERA. Held sex-based classification subject to strict scrutiny under state ERA.

Notes of Interest
Defendant H.D. Gould, Superintendent of Wishkah Valley School District, represented officials of school district and state athletic assn. Landmark equal rights decision—"the exclusion of students from athletic competition solely because of sex, without individual determination of their qualifications violated state ERA." Found no rational relationship between students sex and ability to play football.

Name and Citation
BEDNAR V. NEBRASKA SCHOOL ACTIVITIES ASSOCIATION, 531 F.2nd 922 (8th Cir. 1976)
Date March 11, 1976

Court and Judge
U.S. Ct. Appeals 8th Circuit District Judge Warren Urbom Cir. Judge Lay

Issue and Nature
Ilsa Bednar, a high school 10th grader at Johnson Brock High School challenged an association rule prohibiting mixed competition. District court had already issued preliminary injunction. No girls' team.

Ruling and Statute
Won. In favor of girl. Affirmed courts' decision in which defendants conceded NSAA rule was invalid. Unconstitutional.

Notes of Interest
Granted to prevent irreparable harm in absence of girls' team.

Name and Citation
CARNES V. TENNESSEE SECONDARY ATHLETIC ASSOCIATION, 415 F. Supp. 569 (E.D. Tenn. 1976)
Date May 10, 1976

Court and Judge
U.S.D.C., E.D. Tennessee, Judge Robert L. Taylor

Issue and Nature
18 year old Jo Ann Carnes, high school senior, wanting to play baseball, sought preliminary injunction against TSAA prohibiting enforcement of a rule banning mixed participation in contact sports (of which baseball is so named). Claimant was denied right to participate in interscholastic baseball at Central High School, Wartburg, Tennessee.

Ruling and Statute
Won. In favor of Girl. Preliminary injunction granted.

Notes of Interest
Court questioned reasoning for TSAA rule in that it allows males highly prone to injury and prevents *all* females. Court also questioned baseball as a contact sport.

Name and Citation
JUNIOR FOOTBALL ASSOCIATION OF ORANGE COUNTY, TEXAS V. GAUDET, 546 S.W.2d 70 (1976).

Date 1976

Court and Judge
Court of Civil Appeals of Texas

Issue and Nature
Gaudet, a female athlete, brought a suit seeking a temporary and permanent injunction requiring the Junior Football Association (JFA) to allow girls to participate in football league and was granted injunction. JFA appealed (which is the case cited).

Ruling and Statute
JFA won its appeal. Appeals Court vacated and dissolved the lower court's decision.

Notes of Interest
Court said that "under the law" as written in the Texas Constitution requires that the discrimination complained of is state action or private conduct that is encouraged by, enable by, or closely interrelated in function with state action. Given this interpretation, court found none of these circumstances and therefore injunction did not hold.

Name and Citation
CAPE V. TENNESSEE SECONDARY SCHOOL ATHLETIC ASSOCIATION 424 F. Supp. 732 (E.D. Tennessee 1976) revised per currium, F.2nd. 793 (6th Circuit 1977)

Date Oct. 3, 1977

Court and Judge
U.S.D.C. E.D. Tennessee Judge Robert L. Taylor; U.S. Court of Appeals 6th Circuit Judge Engel

Issue and Nature
Victoria Cape, a junior high school student at Oak Ridge High School and guard on basketball team, contended that 6-player "split-court" rules denied her full benefits of game and prevented her from obtaining a college athletic scholarship.

Ruling and Statute
Lost. In favor of defendants. Reversed district courts' decision to strike rules. Rejected Private Right of Action under Title IX, 14th Amendement.

Notes of Interest
Appeals court concluded girls are less capable athletes than boys and would be eliminated from participation and athletic involvement.

Name and Citation
HOOVER V. MEIKELJOHN, 430 F. Supp. 164 (D. Colo. 1977)

Date April 15, 1977

Court and Judge
U.S.C.D. D. Colorado Judge Matsch

Issue and Nature
16 year old high school junior, Donna Hoover, challenged Colorado High School Athletic Association which limited participation on interscholastic soccer teams to "members of male sex."

Ruling and statute
Won. In favor of girl. 28 U.S.C. 1343 (3)

Notes of Interest
Equal Protection challenge to exclusion of soccer without concern over contact and non-contact. More forthright concerning separate but equal.

Name and Citation
MUSCARE V. O'MALLEY No. 76-C-3729 (No opinion was written since suit was concluded via consent decree).

Date April 26, 1977

Court and Judge
U.S.D.C. N.D. Illinois Judge John F. Gradey

Issue and Nature
12 year old Tina Muscare Alleged that Chicago Park District football program excluded females from tackle program, although does offer touch football program for girls. Plaintiff deserves to play tackle.

Ruling and Statute
Won. In favor of girl. 14th Amendment

Notes of Interest
Courts concluded that offering a sport for males only, while not offering a sport for females, was not equal opportunity. Rule found Unconstitutional.

Name and Citation
JONES V. SECONDARY SCHOOL ACTIVITIES ASSOCIATION, 453 F. Supp. 150 (W.D. Okla., 1977)

Date 1977

Court and Judge
U.S.D.C. W.D. Oklahoma

Issue and Nature
Cheryl Jones was a junior guard on a basketball team in Oklahoma City School System that still went by the girls' rules of basketball, that is, six player, "split-court." She sought a preliminary and permanent injunction to have Association discontinue use of these rules.

Ruling and Statute
Won. In favor of the girl in part 28 U.S.C. 1343 (3,4), 42 U.S.C. 1983, 20 U.S.C. 1681 (Title IX) and 14th Amendment "equal protection."

Notes of Interest
Court dismissed those portions dealing with Title IX on the grounds that plaintiff had not exhausted all administrative remedies. The court held that these rules which might cause reduced opportunity to compete in amateur, professional and Olympic basketball and reduce opportunity for college athletic scholarships do not constitute equal protection deprivation of the 14th Amendment.

Name and Citation

AIKEN V. UNIVERSITY OF OREGON 39 OR App. 779 (1979)

Date Oct. 17, 1977; April 23, 1979

Court and Judge

Court of Appeals of State of Oregon Judge Gillete (in judicial review of Chancellor of State Board of Education).

Issue and Nature

Barbara and Robert Aiken, with two daughters at the University of Oregon on basketball team, charged inequality in four areas of U. of Oregon intercollegiate athletic program: transportation, officiating, coaching and university commitment.

Ruling and Statute

Won. In favor of women. Review Board reversed Chacncellor's Order Maintained original officers' determination that University was in violation of ORS 650.150.

Notes of Interest

Provision says that institution guided by regulations implementing Title IX. Review Board found no support in legislation for R.E. Liuallen's (Chancellor's) determination of a compliance schedule.

Name and Citation

YELLOW SPRINGS EXEMPTED VILLAGE SCHOOL DISTRICT V. OHIO ATHLETIC ASSOCIATION, 433 F. Sup. 753 (S.D. Ohio, 1978)

Date Jan. 9, 1978

Court and Judge

U.S.D.C. S.D. Ohio Judge Carl Rubin

Issue and Nature

In 1974 two female 7th grade students (Leah Wing & Amy Underwood) at Morgan Middle School, competed for and were awarded positions on their school basketball team. But were excluded from team because of rules of Ohio Athletic Association prohibiting mixed sex athletic teams.

Ruling and Statute

Won. In favor of girls. Rule held Unconstitutional.

Notes of Interest

Judge Rubin concluded, "It may well be that there is a student today in Ohio high school who lacks the proper coaching and training to become the greatest quarterback in professional history—of course the odds are astronomical against her, but she is entitled to a fair chance to try."

Name and Citation

LEFFEL V. WISCONSIN INTERSCHOLASTIC ATHLETIC ASSOCIATION, 444 F. Supp. 1117 (E.D. Wisconsin 1978).

Date Jan. 19, 1978

Court and Judge

U.S.D.C. E.D. Wisconsin Judge Myron L. Gordon

Nature and Issue

Challenge to Athletic Association rule which deprives girls the opportunity to play contact sports in mixed competition. Susan Leffel and another Milwaukee High School girl joined their cases. Both had been prohibited from participating on boys' varsity baseball team. Class Action.

Won. In favor of girls. Equal Protection Clause: 14th Amend.; 42 U.S.C. 1983.

Notes of Interest

Contact sport cases are not hopeless, just harder. Did repeat, however, that separate teams satisfy constitutional requirements.

Name and Citation

NATIONAL COLLEGIATE ATHLETIC ASSOCIATION V. CALIFANO 444 F. Supp. 425 (1978), rev'd 622 F.2nd 1382 (1980)

Date 1978; April 18, 1980

Court and Judge

U.S.D.C. (D. Kansas) Judge O'Connor; U.S. Court of Appeals 10th Circuit

Issue and Nature

The NCAA, a voluntary, unincorporated intercollegiate association instituted declaratory and injunctive relief seeking to invalidate regulations promulgated by HEW with respect to sex discrimination in college athletics. The defendant interveners in this case were the Association for Intercollegiate Athletics for Women (AIAW), National Education Association (NEA) and United states Student Association (USSA).

Rulling and Statute

NCAA won right to sue. Reversed District Court's decision that NCAA lacked standing to sue.

Notes of Interest

Appeals Court decision has sent the case back to district court in Kansas City where the NCAA's' original question (as stated in Issue & Nature) will be decided.

Name and Citation

RIDGEFIELD WOMEN'S POLITICAL CAUCUS, INC. V. FOSSI, 458 F. Supp. 117 (1978)

Date 1978

Court and Judge

U.S.D.C. (D. Connecticut)

Issue and Nature

Town selectmen agreed, under contract, to rent public property to private organization, Boys' Club Inc. for a nominal fee ($1.00). Boys' Club Inc. will make a substantial profit on the use of this facility while their programs are restricted to male participation. Ridgefield Political Caucus, Inc., on behalf of the girls and tax paying parents sought an injunction to prevent town selectmen's proposal to convey public property for nominal consideration to a private organization that restricts membership to boys.

Ruling and Statute

Won. In favor of caucus. Injunction granted. 14th Amendment, equal protection clause; 42 U.S.C. 1983; and the state's equivalent to the 14th amendment.

Notes of Interest

Court said that the town selectmen could not constitutionally make proposed conveyance in question.

Name and Citation

HUTCHINS V. BOARD OF TRUSTEES OF MICHIGAN STATE UNIVERSITY
C.A. No. G 79-87

Date Feb. 6, 1979

Court and Judge

U.S.D.C., W.D. Michigan Judge Noel P. Fox

Issue and Nature

Complaint filed by women's basketball team from East Lansing Campus. Charged Michigan State University and Board of Trustees with sex discrimination and flagrant violation of Title IX by giving the men's team "better treatment" (More money for traveling, better facilities, etc.). Trial date pending.

Ruling and Statute

Won. Temporary restraining order issued barring Michigan State from giving its men's basketball team better treatment than its women's teams.

Notes of Interest

Court said "If the girls are going to play a rough game then they do need proper rest and nutrition."

Name and Citation

DODSON V. ARKANSAS ACTIVITIES ASSOCIATION 468 F. Supp. 394 (1979)

Date 1979

Court and Judge

U.S.D.C. (E.D. Arkansas)

Issue and Nature

Dodson, a junior high school basketball player, in a league that uses the girls rules of six-player "split-court" sought an injunction to have the Arkansas Activities Association stop using girls' rule in junior and senior high school programs.

Ruling and Statute

Won. In favor of girl Injunction granted. 14th Amendement, Equal Protection, and Title IX.

Notes of Interest

Court threw out Title IX question saying there was no evidence that any "educational program or activity" involved in the present case received "federal financial assistance." But, the Court ruled that "differences in girls' and boys' Senior and Junior High School basketball rules deprive girls of equal protection of laws." "Gender related substantive reasons were not sufficient justification since such rules place girl athletes in Arkansas at a substantial disadvantage as compared to boy athletes."

Name and Citation
GOMES V. GHODE ISLAND INTERSCHOLASTIC LEAGUE, 469 F. Supp. 659 (1979)

Date 1979

Court and Judge
U.S.D.C. (D. Rhode Island)

Issue and Nature
Gomes, a male athlete in Rhode Island, sought injunctive relief against the school district to allow him to play on an all girls' volleyball team since there was no such team available to boys.

Ruling and Statute
Won. In favor of boy. Preliminary Injuction granted Title IX; 41 U.S.C. 1983; and 14th Amendment, Equal Protection.

Notes of Interest
Court based its decision on "separate but equal," saying that "a qualified male may play on an all girls' athletic team when the high school offers no separate male team."

Name and Citation
PETRIE V. ILLINOIS HIGH SCHOOL ASSOCIATION, 394 N.E.2d 855 (1979)

Date 1979

Court and Judge
Illinois Court of Appeals 4th Circuit

Issue and Nature
Petrie, a male athlete, sought an injunction against the Illinois High School Association in order to allow him to play on the all girls' volleyball team in his school.

Ruling and Statute
Lost. In favor of defendants. Appeals Court affirmed the lower court's decision. Equal Protection under state laws, SHA Constit. 1970 art. 1 18.

Notes of Interest
Court stated that rule did not violate the state constitutional provisions prohibiting state and its units of local government and school districts from denying or abridging equal protection of the laws on account of sex.

Name and Citation
ATTORNEY GENERAL V. MASSACHUSETTS INTERSCHOLASTIC ATH-
LETIC ASSOCIATION, 393 N.E. 2nd 284 (1979)

Date 1979

Court and Judge
Superior Judicial Court of Massachusetts

Issue and Nature

The Attorney General and others were seeking an injunction against Massachusetts Interscholastic Athletic Association rule that no girl could play on a boys' team if that sport was not offered to girls.

Ruling and Statute

Won. Injunction was granted. MGLA 76 5, Constit. P.L. Art. 1, amended Art. 106 and Mass. ERA.

Notes of Interest

Court declared that rule 17(n)(1) was invalid.

Name and Citation

ROBIN V. NEW YORK STATE PUBLIC HIGH SCHOOL ATHLETIC ASSOCIATION, 420 N.Y.S.2d 394 (Appell. Div. 2nd Dept. 1979)

Date Sep. 24, 1979

Court and Judge

Appellate Division 2nd Dept. Judges: O'Connor, Gulotta, Lazer, and Rabin

Issue and Nature

A female athlete, Valerie Robin who had the year before successfully challenged the New York State Public High School Athletic Association's rule prohibiting mixed competition alleged that an athletic association's eligibility rule had been punitively applied against her. She challenged the Athletic Associations' right to punitively apply its rules.

Ruling and Statute

Won. In favor of girl. Athletic association's ruling was declared without sound base.

Notes of Interest

Appellate Division Court ruled that Athletic Association had abused its powers in inflexibly applying rule to high school girl who had been unaware of eligibility requirement.

APPENDIX B
Table of Cases

Albers v. Independent School District No. 302 of Lewis Co.. 94 Idaho 342, 487 P.2d 936 (1971).

Bellman v. San Francisco High School District. 11 Cal.2d 576, 81 P.2d 894 (1938).

Bourque v. Duplechin. 331 S.2d 40 (La. App. 1976).

Brackman v. Adrian. 472 S.W.2d 735 (Tenn. 1971).

Brahatcek v. Millard School District No. 17, 273 N.W.2d 680 (Nebraska 1979.)

Brooks v. Bd. of Education of City of New York. 238 N.Y.S.2d 963, 189 N.E. 2d 497 (1963).

Carabba v. Anacortes School District No. 103. 72 Wash.2d 939, 435 P.2d 936 (1967).

Chatman v. State. 6 Wash. App. 316, 492 P.2d 607 (Wash. Ct. App. 1972).

Cirillo v. City of Milwaukee. 34 Wis.2d 705, 150 N.W.2d 460 (1967).

Clayton, et al. v. New Dreamland Roller Skating Rink. 14 N.J. Super. 390 (1951).

Coddell v. Johnson, Civil Action No. Ca-7-615 (N.D. Tex. June 30, 1972).

Commonwealth. Packel v. Pennsylvania I.A.A., 334 A. 2d 839 (1974).

Curtiss v. Young Men's Christian Association of the Lower Columbia Basin. 82 Wash.2d 455, 511 P.2d 991 (Wash. 1973).

Dailey v. Los Angeles Unified School District. 84 Cal. Rptr. 325, vac. 87 Cal Rptr. 376, 470 P.2d 360 (1970).

Daniel v. S-Co Corp.. 255 Iowa 869, 124 N.W.2d 522 (1963).

Darrin v. Gould. 85 Wash.2d 859, 540 P.2d 882 (1975).

DeGooyer v. Harkness. 70 S.D. 26, 13 N.W.2d 815 (1944).

Dunham v. Pulsifer. 312 F. Supp. 411 (D. Vt. 1970).

Fessenden v. Smith. 255 Iowa 1170, 124 N.W.2d 554 (1964).

Frank v. Orleans Parish School Board. 195 So.2d 451 (La. App. 1967).

Goss v. Lopez. 419 U.S. 565 (1975).

Handy v. Hadley—Luzerne Union Free School District. 277 N.Y. 685, 14 N.E.2d 390, 1938.

Hanson et al.. v. Reedley Joint Union High School District et al.. 43 Ca.2d 643, 111 P.2d 415 (1941).

Jacques v. Lake Placid. 332 N.Y.S.2d 743 (1972).

Jones v. Battles. 315 F. Supp. 601 (D. Conn. 1970).

Keesee v. Bd. of Education of the City of New York. 235 N.Y.S.2d 300 (1962).

Kerby v. Elk Grove Union High School Dist.. 1 Cal. App.2d 246, 36 P.2d 431 (1934).

Kitzel v. Atkeson et al.. 173 Kan. 198, 245 P.2d 170 (1952).

LaValley v. *Stanford*, 70 N.Y.S.2d 460 (1947).

Long v. *Zopp*, 476 F.2d 180 (4th Cir. 1973).

Mailloux v. *Kiley*, 323 F. Supp. 1387 (D. Mass. 1971), aff'd 448 F.2d 1242 (1st Cir. 1971).

Mark v. *Colgate University*, 385 N.Y.S.2d 621 (1976).

Miller v. *Cloidt and Board of Education of the Borough of Chatham*, No. L7241-62 (N.J. Super. Ct. 1964).

Mogabgab v. *Orleans Parish School Board*, La. App., 239 S.2d 456 (1970).

Mokovich v. *Independent School District No. 22*, St. Louis County, 177 Minn. 446, 225 N.W. 292 (1929).

Moran v. *School District No. 7*, Yellowstone County, 350 F. Supp. 1180 D. Mont. 1972).

Nabozny v. *Barnhill*, 31 Ill App.3d 212, 334 N.E.2d 258 (1975).

Olson v. *Nissen Corp.*, Iowa Linn County District Court, L.A. 1284, June 15, 1977.

Perry v. *Seattle School Dist. No. 1*, 66 Wash.2d 800, 405 P.2d 589 (1965).

Pirkle v. *Oakdale Union Grammar School Dist.*, 40 Cal.2d 207, 253 P.2d 1 (1953).

Price v. *Mt. Diablo Unified School Dist.*, 177 Cal. App.2d 312, 2 Cal. Rptr. 23 (1960).

Rodriguez v. *Seattle School District No. 1*, 66 Wash.2d 51, 401 P.2d 326 (1965).

Sayers v. *Ranger*, 83 A.2d 775 (N.H. Super. Ct., 1951).

Scala v. *City of New York*, 102 N.Y. Supp.2d 790 (Sup. Ct. 1951.)

Stanley v. *Bd. of Education of the City of Chicago*, 9 Ill. App.3d 963, 293 N.E.2d 417 (1973).

Stevens v. *Central School Dist. No. 1 of the Town of Ramapo*, 270 N.Y.S.2d 23, aff'd 21 N.Y.2d 780, 288 N.Y.S.2d 475, 235 N.E.2d 448.

Styer v. *Reading*, 360 Pa. 212, 61 A.2d 382 (1948).

Summers v. *Milwaukie Union High School District No. 5*, Or App. 196, 481 P.2d 369 (1971).

Sunday v. *Stratton Corp.*, 136 Vt. 293, 390 A.2d 398, (1978).

Tinker v. *Des Moines School District*, 393 U.S. 503 (1969).

Vendrell v. *School Dist. No. 26C Malheur County*, 226 Ore. 263, 360 P.2d 282 (1961).

Welch v. *Dunsmuir Joint Union High School District*, 326 P.2d 633 (Cal App. 1958).

Wright v. *Mt. Mansfield Lift*, 96 F. Supp. 786, (D. Vt. 1951).

Wright v. *San Bernardino High School District*, 121 Cal. App.2d 342, 263 P.2d 25 (1953).

APPENDIX C
Selected Bibliography

BOOKS

American Alliance for Health, Physical Education and Recreation. *Selected Problems in Sport Safety.* Washington, D.C.: AAHPER Publications, 1975. 91 pp.

Appenzeller, Herb. *Athletics and the Law.* Charlottseville, Va.: The Michie Company, 1978. 262 pp.

Appenzeller, Herb. *Physical Education and the Law.* Charlottesville, Va.: The Michie Company, 1978. 185 pp.

Cocci, Michel A., John W. Dondanville, and Thomas R. Nelson, *Product Liability. Trends and Implications.* New York: American Management Association, 1970. 71 pp.

Delon, Floyd G. *Substantive Legal Aspects of Teacher Discipline.* Topeka: National Organization on Legal Problems of Education, 1972.

Drury, Robert L. *Essentials of School Law.* New York: Appleton-Century-Crofts. 1967. 215 pp.

Edwards, Newton. *The Courts and the Public Schools; the Legal Basis of School Organization and Administration.* Chicago: University of Chicago Press, 1971. 710 pp.

Gerlach, Ronald A., and Lynne W. Lamprecht. *Teaching About the Law.* Cincinnati: The W.H. Anderson Company, 1975. 354 pp.

Gray, Irwin. *Product Liability: A Management Response.* New York: American Management Association, 1975. 239 pp.

Grieve, Andrew. *The Legal Aspects of Athletics.* New York: A.S. Barnes and Co., 1969. 183 pp.

Hazard, William R., Lawrence D. Freeman, Stephen Eisdorfer, and Paul Tractenberg. *Legal Issues in Teacher Preparation and Certification.* Washington, D.C.: ERIC Clearinghouse on Teacher Eduction, 1977. 151 pp.

Hazard, William R. *Education and the Law.* 2nd ed. New York: The Free Press, 1978. 606 pp.

Hooker, Clifford P. and Kenneth J. ReHage, (eds.). *The Courts and Education.* Chicago: National Society for the Study of Education: distributed by the University of Chicago Press, 1978. 389 pp.

Hudgins, H.C. Jr., and Richard S. Vacca. *Law and Education: Contemporary Issues and Court Decisions.* Charlottesville, Va: The Michie Company, 1979. 364 pp.

Levine, Alan H. and Eve Cary. *The Rights of Students.* New York: Avon Books, 1977. 149 pp.

Nolte, M. Chester, and John Phillip Linn. *School Law for Teachers.* Danville, Illinois; Interstate Printers and Publishers, 1963. 343 pp.

Piele, Philip K. and James R. Forsberg. *School Property: The Legality of its Use and Disposition.* Topeka: National Organization on Legal Problems of Education, 1974.

Prosser, William L. *Handbook of the Law of Torts.* 4th ed. St. Paul, Minn.: West Publishing Co., 1971. 1208 pp.

Punke, Harold H. *Law and Liability in Pupil Transportation.* Chicago: The University of Chicago Press, 1943. 289 pp.

Reasons, Charles E., and Robert M. Rich. *The Sociology of Law.* Toronto, Canada: Butterworth and Co., 1978. 475 pp.

Reutter, E. Edmund, Jr. *Legal Aspects of Control of Student Activities by Public School Authorities.* Topeka: National Organization on Legal Problems of Education, 1974.

Reutter, E. Edmund, Jr. *The Courts and Student Conduct.* Topeka: National Organization on Legal Problems of Education, 1975.

Rubin, David. *The Rights of Teachers.* New York: Avon Books, 1968. 176 pp.

Van der Smissen, Betty. *Legal Liability of Cities and Schools for Injuries in Recreation and Parks.* Cincinnati: The W.H. Anderson Company, 1968. Separate 1975 Supplement. 402 pp.

Weistart, John C. and Cym H. Lowell. *The Law of Sports.* Indianapolis: Bobbs-Merrill Company, 1979. 1154 pp.

ARTICLES

Allen, R.B. "Lawyers, Law, and Baseball." *American Bar Association Journal* 64 (October, 1978), pp. 1530-1535.

Arnold, D.E. "Compliance with Title IX in Secondary School Physical Education." *JOPER* 48 (Jan. 1977), pp. 19-22.

Arnold, D.E. "Sports Product Liability." *JOPER* 49 (Nov.-Dec. 1978), pp. 25-28.

"Athletics." *Law and Contemporary Problems* 38, no. 1 (Winterspring 1973) 171 pp.

Bain, L.L. "Implementing Title IX: Concern of Undergraduate Physical Education Majors." *JOPER* 50 (Nov.-Dec. 1979), p. 77.

Baker, B.B. "Legal Implications Concerning the Use of Physical Therapy Modalities by Athletic Trainers," *Journal of the National Athletic Trainers Association.* 10 No. 4 (Dec. 1975).

Bird, P.J. and Gansneder, B.M. "Preparation of Physical Education Teachers as Required Under Public Law 94-142." *Exceptional Children* 45 (March 1979), pp. 464-466.

Carpenter, L.J., and R.V. Acosta. "Violence in Sport—Is It Part of the Game or the Intentional Tort of Battery?" *JOPER* 51 (Sept. 1980). pp. 18.

Carrafiello, V.A. "Jocks are People too: The Constitution Comes to the Locker Room." *Creighton Law Review* 13 (Spring 1980), pp. 843-862.

Chambless, J.R. and C.J. Mangin. "Legal Liability and the Physical Educator." *JOHPER.* 44 (April 1973) p. 42.

Drowatzky, J.N. "On the Firing Line: Negligence in Physical Education." *Journal of Law and Eduction* 6 (Oct. 1977), pp. 481-490.

Drowatzky, J.N. "Cooperating Teacher and Liability during Student Teacher Supervision. *JOPER* 51 (Feb. 1980), pp. 79-80.

Dunn, R.S., and R.W. Cole. "Inviting Malpractice through Mainstreaming" *Educational Leadership* 36 (Feb. 1979) pp. 302-306.

Eberlein, L. "Teacher in the Courtroom: New Role Expectation?" *The Clearing House* 53 (Feb. 1980), pp. 287-291.

Ecker, T. "Will We Allow the Courts to Kill Sports?" *Athletic Journal* 57 (May, 1977), pp. 12-13.

Frakt, A.N. Adventure Programming and Legal Liability." *JOPER* 49 (April 1978) pp. 49-51.

Frazier, C.S. "Sports Litigation! The New Attitude." *Coach and Athlete*   41 (May-June 1979), p. 11.

Frazier, C.S. "Coaches Legally Accountable to Athletes." *Coach and Athlete* 40 (April 1978), p. 14.

Gallagher, M.R. "Players vs. Physicians: The Legal Season May be Ready to Open." *The Physician and Sports Medicine.* 1 (June 1973), p. 56.

Gregory, I.F.II , and A. Goldsmith. "The Sports Spectator as Plaintiff." *Trial* 16 (March 1980), pp. 26-29.

Hammes, R.P. "Tort and the Teacher: Some Considerations." *The Clearing House* 53 (October 1979), pp. 104-108.

Hechter, W. "Criminal Law and Violence in Sports." *Criminal Law Quarterly* 19 (Summer 1977), pp. 425-453.

Herbert, W.G. and D.L. Herbert. "Legal Aspects of Physical Fitness Testing." *JOPER* 46 (June 1975), pp. 17-19.

"High School Athletics and Due Process: Notice of Eligibility Rules." *Nebraska Law Review.* 57 (1978), pp. 877-892.

Horgan, J.S. and D.L. Porretta. "Model Staff Development Program for Implementing P.L. 94-142 in Physical Education." *JOPER* 50 (March 1979), pp. 35-36.

Hurt, W.T. "Elements of Tort Liability as Applied to Athletic Injuries." *Journal of School Health* 46 (April 1976), pp. 200-203.

Hutter, D.M. "Legal Liability in Physical Education and Athletics." *Physical Educator* 35 (October 1975), pp. 160-163.

"Injuries Resulting from Nonintentional Acts in Organized Contact Sports: The Theories of Recovery Available to the Injured Athlete." *Indiana Law Review* 12 (April 1979), pp. 687-711.

Jensen, J.E. "Title IX and Intercollegiate Athletics: HEW Gets Serious About Equality in Sports?" *New England Law Review* 15 (Summer 1979-80), pp. 573-596.

Kazmaier, R.W. "Naked Truth About Sports: Product Liability." *Scholastic Coach* 47 (May 1978), pp. 26-27.

Kelley, B.J. "Implementing Title IX." *JOPER* 48 (February 1977), pp. 27-8.

McCarthy, M.M. "Tort Liability." *Yearbook of School Law* 1978, pp. 237-276.

McDaniel, T.R. "Corporal Punishment and Teacher Liability." *The Clearing House* 54 (September 1980), pp. 10-13.

McGreevy, M. "Litigation and the Courts." *Scholastic Coach* 50 (November 1980), p. 6.

Narol, M.S. and S. Dedopoulos, "Kill the Umpire: A Guide to Referees' Rights." *Trial* 15 (March 1979), pp. 32-34.

Narol, M.S. and S. Dedopoulos. "Defamation: A Guide to Referees' Rights." *Trial* 16 (January 1980), pp. 42-44 also *Trial* 16 (March 1980), pp. 18-21.

Ostro, H. "Legal Liability and the Athletic Director." *Scholastic Coach* 49 (May-June 1980), p. 8.

Parsons, T.W. "What Price Prudence?" *JOPER* 50 (January 1979), p. 45.

"Participants Liability for Injury to a Fellow Participant in an Organized Athletic Event." *Chicago-Kent Law Review* 53 (1976), pp. 97-108.

Peterson, T.L. and S.A. Smith. "The Role of the Lawyer on the Playing Field: Sports Injury Litigation." *Barrister* 7 (Summer 1980), p. 10.

Pitt, M.B. "Malpractice on the Sidelines: Developing a Standard of Care for Team Sport Physicians." *COMM-ENT* 2 (Spring 1980), pp. 579-600.

Rankin, J.S. "Legal System as a Proponent of Adventure Programming." *JOPER* 49 (April 1978), pp. 52-53.

Richardson, R.C. Jr., and E. Johnson. "Narrowing the Limits of Administrative Discretion." *Peabody Journal of Education* 58 (October 1980), pp. 22-26.

"Sex Discrimination in Interscholastic High School Athletics." *Syracuse Law Review* 25 (Spring 1974), pp. 535-574.

"Sexual Equality in High School Athletics: The Approach of Darrin v. Gould." *Gonzaga Law Review* 12 (Summer 1977), pp. 691-706.

"Sports and the Law." *Trial* 14 (June 1978), pp. 24-32.

"Sports Litigation." *Trial* 13 (January 1977), pp. 21-29.

Thurston, P.W."Torts" *Yearbook of School Law* 1980, pp. 231-267.

"Tort Liability for Players in Contact Sports." *University of Missouri-Kansas City Law Review* 45 (Fall 1976), pp. 119-129.

Tractenberg, P.L. "Reply to Inviting Malpractice through Mainstreaming." *Educational Leadership* 36 (February 1979), pp. 306-307.

"True Story of What Happens When the Big Kids Say 'It's my football, and you'll either play by my rules or you won't play at all.' " *Nebraska Law Review* 55 (1976), pp. 335-361.

Tucher, N.R. "Assumption of Risk and Vicarious Liability in Personal Injury Actions Brought by Professional Athletes." *Duke Law Journal* September 1980, pp. 742-765.

DISSERTATIONS

Arnold, Donald Eugene. "Legal Basis of Physical Education in Selected States." P.E.D. Dissertation, Indiana University, 1971. 302 pp.

Baker, Boyd B. "Physical Education and the Law: A proposed Course for the Professional Preparation of Physical Educators." Ph.D. Dissertation, the University of Oregon, 1971. 129 pp.

Bartman, Robert Earl. "The Legal Status of Academic Freedom in the Public Schools." Ed.D. Dissertation, The University of Missouri-Columbia, 1975. 178 pp.

Benson, Michael Arthur. "The Legal Status of Student Activity Fees and Policies Regarding Their Use in Elected Institutions of Higher Learning." Ed.D. Dissertation, The University of Georgia, 1977. 130 pp.

Cox, John Owen. "The Impact of Legal Decisions Rendered from 1970-76 Pertaining to State Athletic Association and Public School Board Eligibility Rules for Student Participation in Athletics." Ph.D. Dissertation, Iowa State University, 1976. 119 pp.

Harvey, A. Neil. "Legal Aspects Governing the Organization and Control of the Pennsylvania Interscholastic Athletic Association in It's Role with Pennsylvania's Public and Private Schools." Ed.D. Dissertation, Temple University, 1976. 277 pp.

Hopkins, Vicki Lyn. "Legal Liability in Physical Education from 1966 to 1976." Ph.D. Dissertation, University of Utah, 1978. 185 pp.

Koehler, Robert. "A Study of Legal Liability with Emphasis on Physical Education in Selected States from 1955 to 1965." Ed.D. Dissertation, The University of Utah, 1967. 135 pp.

Martin, David V. "Trends in Tort Liability of School District as Revealed by Court Decisions." Ed.D. Dissertation, Duke University, 1962. 276 pp.

Meggelin, Gary P. "A Case Law Handbook for Montana School Administrators." Ed.D. Dissertation, University of Montana, 1979. 230 pp.

Mohler, J. David. "Legal Aspects of Extracurricular Activities in Secondary Schools." Ed.D. Dissertation, Duke University, 1965. 258 pp.

Nash, Herbert Dallas. "A Survey of Professional Opinion on the Legal, Financial, and Program Provisions and Expected Impact of Provisions Contained in Public Law 94-142 on State and Local Programs for the Handicapped." Ed.D. Dissertation, The University of Georgia, 1978. 168 pp.

Russell, William Leonard. "The Legal Aspects of Girls Interscholastic Athletics." Ed.D. Dissertation, The University of North Carolina at Greensboro, 1978. 340 pp.

Schroyer, George F. "Requirements, Legal Implications and a Teacher's Guide for Physical Education in Secondary Schools." Ph.D. Dissertation, The University of Wyoming, 1963. 72 pp.

Soich, John E. "Analysis of Tort Liability of School Districts and/or its Officers, Agents, and Employees in Conducting Programs of Physical Education, Recreation and Athletics." Ed.D. Dissertation, The University of Pittsburgh, 1964. 259 pp.

INDEX

150   INDEX